Expanded Praise for
Gen X: The X Factor for Growth

"With *Gen X: The X Factor for Growth*, Mary Ellen and Julia shine a spotlight on a generation too often overlooked yet crucial to today's business success. Their sharp insights and actionable strategies are a game changer for organizations seeking to drive growth with this powerhouse demographic. This book is as compelling as it is practical—don't miss it."

—Todd Unger, Chief Experience Officer of the American Medical Association and International Best-Selling Author of *The 10-Second Customer Journey*

"Mary Ellen and Julia bring a new, valuable perspective to understanding and unlocking the potential of Gen X for business growth. The book is a great resource for leaders."

—Jason Dorsey, President of The Center for Generational Kinetics and Best-Selling Author of *Zconomy*

"*Gen X: The X Factor for Growth* proves that this overlooked generation is a significant part of our population. It is a marketing guide to taking back the lost generation and becoming a powerhouse that provides answers to their needs."

—Kristen Cavallo, Executive Director of The Branch Museum of Design and former Global CEO of MullenLowe Group

"Julia and Mary Ellen brilliantly reveal how Gen X drives leadership, innovation and growth in today's dynamic workforce. As an Executive Coach to senior execs, I see the potential this generation holds to drive even more growth—this book is a game changer for businesses ready to embrace this cohort."

**—Lisa Lanier, CEO & Founder,
Lanier Leadership Group**

GEN X

GEN X

THE X FACTOR FOR GROWTH

**Mary Ellen Dugan
& Julia Fitzgerald**

Redwood
Publishing

Published by
Redwood Publishing, LLC
www.redwooddigitalpublishing.com
Orange County, California

ISBN: 978-1-966333-07-4 (hardcover)
ISBN: 978-1-966333-08-1 (paperback)
ISBN: 978-1-966333-09-8 (e-book)

Cover Design: Michelle Manley, GraphiqueDesigns
Interior Formatting: Creative Publishing Book Design
Interior Graphics: Jtran. (Data/sources utilized to design are properly cited within text and/or caption of graphic.)

Table of Contents

INTRODUCTION   X Marks the Spot   1

PART 1
The Lost Generation and Missed Opportunity

CHAPTER 1   Who Is Gen X?   11

CHAPTER 2   The OG Digital Natives   35

CHAPTER 3   Money Matters   67

CHAPTER 4   The Sandwich Generation   87

PART 2
Tapping Into the X Factor:
The Super Categories and Winning Strategies

CHAPTER 5   The Midlife Categories That Count   113

CHAPTER 6   Work   117

CHAPTER 7   Wealth   143

CHAPTER 8   Wellness   167

CHAPTER 9   Gen Xers Living Their Best Lives   193

CHAPTER 10   Gen Xcellerators   211

CONCLUSION   The Power of the Gen X Market   233

X Marks the Spot

"Don't You (Forget About Me)"

—Simple Minds (1985)

Remember the original Sony PlayStation or rocking out to Nirvana and Pearl Jam? If you are part of Generation X, born between 1965 and 1980, these were likely quintessential parts of your childhood and youth. Often overshadowed by the larger Baby Boomer generation before them and the Millennials who came after, Gen Xers have been dubbed the "latchkey kids" and the "lost generation." However, they are a digital human force to be reckoned with—the first to grow up with video games, computers, and cable TV, while also being the last generation raised largely without ubiquitous internet and mobile devices. Today they have grown up to be a significant part of our population, economy, and the leaders of companies and C-suites across the country.

There's plenty of nostalgia-rich entertainment rooted in Gen X "back in the day" lore but less focus on their current significance. Somehow, the image of Gen X got stuck in the past with the Brat Pack in *The Breakfast Club*. (Cue up the Simple Minds song.) When was the last time you read a business story about Gen X or saw a celebrated marketing campaign targeted to them? Right. You haven't.

Perhaps it's because they have been stereotyped as the cynical slacker kids who came of age between vast cultural and technological shifts. Whatever the reason, this is a generation of tastemakers and trendsetters who helped define American pop culture over the past few decades through trends like grunge rock, indie films, tech entrepreneurship, and more. Just look at some Gen X icons who've left an indelible mark: musicians such as Kurt Cobain, Tupac, and Beastie Boys; writers such as J. K. Rowling, David Sedaris, and Jhumpa Lahiri; celebrity entrepreneurs and executives such as Jay-Z, Larry Page, Sheryl Sandberg, and Elon Musk.

And the numbers tell an impressive economic Gen X narrative. This group is around 65 million people strong, making up almost 20% of the US population—a viable chunk that we cannot afford to ignore. And perhaps most importantly, Gen Xers currently hold an estimated $2.4 trillion in spending power. That number is expected to grow to $4.2 trillion by 2030 as this generation enters their peak earning years. To put that in perspective, Gen X's spending power will eclipse that of Millennials despite the younger cohort's larger population size.

Gen X is projected to inherit a staggering $27 trillion in wealth from Baby Boomers over the next decade, adding to their own earning potential. Despite this massive pending transfer of assets, businesses still tend to focus their marketing efforts on Millennials and Gen Z. This seems like a huge mistake because Gen X has plenty of economic clout of their own.

So, what's the deal? Why are so many businesses overlooking this opportunity?

That is the question posed by Mary Ellen Dugan and Julia Fitzgerald, two research-savvy marketing executives. They are the ultimate authorities—a dynamic duo who have been building business-to-business (B2B) and business-to-consumer (B2C) brands and moving product for decades. With their combined years of hard-won insights working with iconic brands across industries, they have built careers spotting trends and identifying X Factors to grow businesses.

Mary Ellen Dugan has been rocking the B2B CMO and marketing leader role for two decades. After mastering research-backed branding as a practice lead at WPP's Landor Group, she became a marketing expert in digital informed growth platforms. On the cutting edge of technology marketing, Mary Ellen orchestrated game-changing initiatives for brands including Dell Technologies, Indeed, WP Engine, and Envestnet, driving millions in revenue through authentic customer connections and brand experience. She has spearheaded four generational research studies and executive-produced the award-winning documentary *makeSHIFT,* which examines ever-changing digital technology trends.

Julia has been a powerhouse B2C CMO and brand strategist for over 20 years, leading turnarounds and fostering brand affinity everywhere from beloved toy companies to Fortune 100 retailers. Named one of Brand Innovators' Most Influential CMOs, she cut her teeth at Hallmark before leading well-known brands such as VTech, Kmart, Sylvan Learning, Thermos, American Lung Association, and Build-A-Bear to new heights via her uncanny ability to connect with consumers. Author of *Midsize,* Julia shares strategies for successful marketing in midmarket companies in this Amazon best-selling book.

Mary Ellen earned her MBA from NYU's Stern School of Business and Julia received her MBA from the Kellogg

School of Management, but these two Buckeyes started their journey on the same campus at the Max M. Fisher College of Business, Ohio State University's business school. Aligned with their Big 10 business degrees and Midwestern sense of practicality and humor, these two traded insights and wisdom throughout their career paths. It's not surprising they ended up at a CMO Gen Z roundtable together, asking each other, "Does the world really need one more Gen Z marketing initiative?" Acknowledging the obvious—"No, the topic's been covered!"—they started talking about Mary Ellen's generational research and the curious dearth of focus on Gen X. And they kept building on that reality.

With their complementary expertise and chemistry, Mary Ellen and Julia are the perfect partners to lay out actionable strategies for tapping into Gen X's unparalleled influence as consumers, culture-shapers, and decision-makers. This book is a rallying cry from two respected veterans who know what it really takes to win loyalty from this often-overlooked powerhouse generation. They make an airtight case for why businesses simply cannot afford to ignore the X Factor of Gen X any longer.

In this book, Mary Ellen and Julia will go beyond the stereotypes that have pigeonholed Gen X as the cynical slacker kids who grew up as latchkey loners. The truth is, they came of age between analog and digital worlds, becoming the original "digital natives." But that formative experience didn't make them lazy or aloof; it made them uniquely resilient, adaptable, and able to navigate a dynamic digital work environment.

Readers will gain an understanding of how Gen X's unique hybrid analog-digital upbringing shaped a singular worldview—an ability to seamlessly navigate and set the tone across multiple realms. They are the essential bridge between the rigid technological immigrants of previous generations and the new digital natives who follow. Their code-switching adaptability makes Gen X the indispensable interface for any enterprise. This book goes beyond misconceptions to reveal Gen X as they really are: a galvanizing force of hardworking innovators, trailblazers, and cultural catalysts who are just hitting their career and income peaks. It will dive deep into what truly defines and drives this generation, exploring the values, habits, cultural touchpoints, and collective consciousness that have powered their irreplaceable influence.

Gen X: The X Factor for Growth also, importantly, looks at Gen X in the here and now. At the time of publishing, Gen Xers are mostly between 45 and 60 years old. Their spending habits cross a range of categories spanning numerous services and products. Travel, financial planning, consumer electronics, and performance apparel are just a few categories where they over-index. Spoiler alert: Their apparel interest has expanded beyond flannel shirts. This is a market segment that is planning for their futures, providing for their families, and often helping with their own aging parents. They have very clear consumer needs and wants, and as a generation, they have the financial means to pursue them.

Packed with real-world examples, deep quantitative research, and market observations, this is more than a book; it's also an empowering manifesto for Gen X itself and proof that this generation is the ultimate X Factor that businesses need to unlock new growth during an era of rapid technological disruption.

Neither Mary Ellen nor Julia is suggesting your company ditch its Gen Z marketing plan or pitches. Instead, this book suggests that there may be an even more lucrative marketing segment you have overlooked. Their point is, focusing on the crowd with the platinum credit cards and the motivation to spend could produce a higher yield for your efforts. With Gen Z kids of their own, both Mary Ellen and Julia can attest that these bright-eyed youngsters are still largely in their "salad days." And many of Gen Z's big-ticket needs and wants are being funded by Gen X.

The first half of the book will focus on insights into Gen X and why it is important for businesses to acknowledge these factors to unlock X Factor growth in their revenues. The second half will focus on areas where the Gen X impact is exceptionally powerful: **WEALTH**, **WORK**, and **WELLNESS**. It will also focus on communication imperatives and how to reach this 65-million-strong powerhouse. You'll find success stories, supported by interviews with experts and practitioners who are effectively leveraging this generation, that you can apply to your own business.

Consider this book your X-ray vision into the opportunity that is sitting right there in the data for your use. You can capitalize on Gen X's still-expanding economic impact and unlock transformative growth opportunities.

Gen X Voices Inspiring the X Factor Conversation

"If I hear one more conference about what Gen Z wants, I'm going to lose it. I'm still paying for my Gen Zer's phone bill and insurance. Why don't they start asking what *I* want?"

—*GEN X MARKETER, MOM OF A 24-YEAR-OLD*

"TikTok has convinced my 13-year-old daughter that she needs top-shelf skin care from Drunk Elephant. Why would I buy her that when I don't pay those prices for myself?"

—*GEN X MOM OF A TEENAGER*

"I invested the time to learn how to code, so I am the first person to see how development timelines can be improved with AI eliminating the need for it."

—*GEN X IT DIRECTOR, AGE 49*

"This is the year we're going to Machu Pichu. Last year was the Northern Boundary Waters. I want to keep scheduling the more intense physical trips while we're in great physical condition."

—*GEN X LANDSCAPE DESIGNER, AGE 57*

PART 1

The Lost Generation and Missed Opportunity

CHAPTER 1

Who Is Gen X?

"Smells Like Teen Spirit"
—Nirvana (1991)

As the iconic opening riff of Nirvana's "Smells Like Teen Spirit" blared from radios and MTV in the fall of 1991, it heralded not just a new sound but the arrival of a generation. Generation X (Gen X)—born between 1965 and 1980—came of age in the shadow of the Baby Boomers but emerged to put their own indelible stamp on American culture and the economy. From the days when they smelled like "teen spirit" to today when they are more likely to smell like suburbia, it's useful to understand Gen X's core influences and how those play out today.

The songs we listen to, TV shows and movies we watch, and cultural milestones we witness leave an indelible mark on every generation. They affect the way we perceive and interact with the world. Only by delving deeper into the influences that shaped and inspired Gen X can we begin to understand their defining traits and preferences, unlocking the secrets of how to market to them. In this chapter, we'll do exactly that.

The Experiences That Define a Generation

While generations are usually defined by the birth dates of the population, the exact dates may vary based on the specific research. Generational personality comes from events that a generation of people experience as they grow up at a certain time in a society's history. In short, generations are defined by shared experiences.

While generations are shaped by the events and cultural moments of their youth, Gen X's experience is unique in a few aspects. First, they are the generation straddling the analog and digital worlds. They were the last to grow up without the internet but the first to navigate the World Wide Web as teens and young adults. They are the original digital natives and technology adopters. Second, as children, they were the original latchkey kids, with rising divorce rates and working mothers giving them a level of self-reliance that became a Gen X hallmark.

But to understand this generation's worldview, it is key to understand the events that impacted them during their childhood and adult life.

Some of the defining events for Gen X include the following:

- The Space Shuttle Challenger disaster (1986)
- The fall of the Berlin Wall (1989)
- Exxon Valdez oil tanker spill (1989)
- The Los Angeles Riots (1992)
- Operation Desert Storm (1991)
- The O. J. Simpson trial (1994–1995)
- The Columbine High School massacre (1999)
- September 11 terrorist attacks (2001)

These momentous events, experienced primarily via television, shaped Gen X's worldview, fostering a sense of skepticism and mistrust of institutions. Truly, every aspect of society, from government and war to the environment, violence, and race, was upended during their formative years. At the same time, growing up in the 1970s and 1980s, the final decades of the Cold War, instilled a sense that America's dominance and prosperity could not be taken for granted.

> **"When we look at generations, they are clues—not a box, and they are driven by trends that we can study."**
>
> —JASON DORSEY, PRESIDENT, RESEARCHER & SPEAKER FOR GENERATIONAL KINETICS

Economic events were also formative and reinforced a sense of caution and pragmatism. With the stock market crash referred to as "Black Monday" in October 1987, the Dow Jones Industrial Average unexpectedly lost almost 22% in a single day. Despite the massive losses, the stock market recovered much of the loss rather quickly, gaining back 57% after just two sessions.[1] However, there was still some job market fallout. Gen Xers were either impacted by a tough job market or they watched their parents struggle to recoup their savings. More importantly, the crash ushered in a period of job insecurity, with companies restructuring and hedging against uncertainty with widespread layoffs. The subdued economy led many Gen Xers to realize that corporate loyalty and job security, which previous generations took for granted, were eroding. Gen X's attitude toward corporate security has remained cautious as layoffs have become more typical and cyclical throughout their careers. Even today, with current waves of layoffs in the tech sector, Gen X employees are less likely to be taken by surprise than junior staffers from younger generations. (More on this topic in Chapter 3.)

Later, as working adults, Gen Xers would also be impacted by the Great Recession of 2007–2009, triggered by the collapse of the housing market. This event resulted in job losses and decreased home equity, and it left a dent in their retirement savings. It also fostered a sense of caution when it comes to future financial planning and a desire to enlist professional help.

The Music That Defined Gen X

Not all the generational influences were traumatic events! Every generation has its signature music. According to research, the music that defines us is the music we listen to from age 12 through 22. During this period, our brains undergo rapid neurological development. The music we love during these years tends to become wired into our memory and emotions. These songs hold disproportionate power over our feelings, and our brains remain connected to them as we age.[2]

While Baby Boomers had the Beatles and the Summer of Love, Gen X built its identity around grunge, hip-hop, and indie films. Nirvana, Pearl Jam, Tupac, Biggie Smalls, and the Beastie Boys formed the soundtrack of their youth.

For Gen Xers, the teenage years spanned the late1970s to the mid-1990s, a period of incredible musical diversity and innovation. While grunge and hip-hop are often cited as the defining sounds of the generation, the reality is more complex. Gen X came of age during the birth of MTV, the rise of alternative rock, the golden age of hip-hop, and the emergence of electronic dance music.

In the early 1980s, Gen X teenagers were tuning into the New Wave sounds of Duran Duran, Depeche Mode, and the Cure, as well as the post-punk of R.E.M. and the Smiths. Madonna, Michael Jackson, Whitney Houston, and Prince dominated the pop charts, while Metallica and Guns N' Roses brought a harder edge to rock. Hip-hop was also making its mark, with Run-DMC, the Beastie Boys, and Public Enemy bringing the genre into the mainstream.

As the decade progressed, alternative rock began to take center stage. Bands including Pixies, Sonic Youth, and Dinosaur Jr. laid the groundwork for the grunge explosion of the early 1990s. Nirvana's *Nevermind,* released in 1991, was a seismic shift, bringing alternative rock into the mainstream and defining the sound of a generation. Pearl Jam, Soundgarden, and Alice in Chains followed, cementing Seattle, at least for the time, as the center of the music world.

At the same time, hip-hop was entering its golden age. Artists such as Tupac, Biggie Smalls, Nas, and Jay-Z were redefining the genre with their gritty, realistic portrayals of urban life. The West Coast sound, pioneered by Dr. Dre and Snoop Dogg, brought gangsta rap to the forefront.

The other Gen X change is *how* they listened to music. The oldest Gen Xers started off with vinyl that they either bought for themselves or inherited from parents or siblings. This gave them an appreciation for the physicality of music and the ritual of dropping the needle onto the record and understanding the importance of the "B-side." Then, cassette tapes became the next popular music format. Many a Gen Xer can relate to the frustration of trying to untangle and rewind that semi-delicate media. (Seriously, if you need a targeted universal trigger for *Aggghhh!,* show the Gen Xer with a pencil in the tape hole trying to rewind it!) However, cassette tapes also gave rise to the beloved mix tape. It quickly became the favorite way to share favorite songs and let that special person know that you *for sure* wanted to date them. The rise of the Sony Walkman accelerated the convenience of portable music as that contraption became *the* must-have item.

As Gen X aged, compact discs (CDs) emerged as the dominant music format. CDs provided better sound quality and durability than cassettes. They also represented the last form of physical media before the transition to digital music. Some Gen Xers were early adopters of MP3 players and online music-sharing platforms in the late 1990s. Ever wonder how many Gen Xers had a dog named Napster? This blend of music and technology is another example of how this generation has systematically adopted digital innovations.

Why the Music Matters Today

The music of Gen X's youth isn't just a nostalgic footnote; it continues to shape the cultural landscape. Many of the artists who defined the generation are still actively touring and releasing music. Radiohead, Missy Elliott, and Jay-Z are just a few examples of Gen X icons who continue to be relevant and influential.

Moreover, the music of Gen X has been passed down to their Millennial and Gen Z children. Musical artists such as Nirvana, Beastie Boys, and Tupac have become multigenerational touchstones, their music discovered and loved anew by each successive generation. This phenomenon isn't just cultural; it is also economic. Catalog music (older songs) now accounts for 69% of music consumption.[3]

For businesses, understanding the enduring appeal of Gen X music is key to connecting with this powerful consumer group. Whether it's using a Smashing Pumpkins song in an Apple iPhone ad, selecting Gwen Stefani as a judge on *The Voice*, or creating exclusive content with '80s and '90s bands for Spotify, tapping into Gen X's musical DNA can be a way to forge an authentic emotional connection.

Marketers often seek evidence to help them select the ideal music to promote their products. Ethnicity, social class, and/ or personality type can distinguish individual music tastes, but age and nostalgia may be the largest determinant of all.

Gen X's musical journey is a testament to the generation's diversity, creativity, and lasting influence. From grunge to gangsta rap, alternative rock to electronic dance music, the sounds of their youth continue to reverberate through the culture. As Gen Xers enter their prime spending years, the music that defined them is more than just a memory; it is also a powerful tool for understanding and engaging this vital group.

Gen X Movies and Influences

Gen X ushered in not only new genres of music but also a new style of film that reflected the zeitgeist. This is wholly consistent with the many changes Gen X adopted across multiple platforms. This is also good context for the content and themes that still resonate today.

The Brat Pack and *The Breakfast Club*

No discussion of Gen X cinema would be complete without mentioning the Brat Pack, a group of young actors who frequently appeared together in coming-of-age films in the 1980s. The core members included Emilio Estevez, Anthony Michael Hall, Rob Lowe, Andrew McCarthy, Demi Moore, Judd Nelson, Molly Ringwald, and Ally Sheedy.

The quintessential Brat Pack film is *The Breakfast Club* (1985), directed by John Hughes. The movie follows five high school students from different cliques who spend a Saturday in detention together. As they interact, they break down stereotypes and discover they have more in common than they thought. The film resonated with Gen X audiences, capturing the angst, alienation, and desire for connection that many experienced in their teenage years.

Other notable Brat Pack films include *St. Elmo's Fire* (1985), *Pretty in Pink* (1986), and *Ferris Bueller's Day Off* (1986). These movies, with their mix of humor, heart, and honest portrayal of teenage life, became touchstones for the generation.

"If I meet someone who hasn't seen a John Hughes movie or even know who he is, I know I don't have to waste my time being their friend."

—GEN XER, AGE 56

Reality Bites and the Slacker Aesthetic

As Gen X moved into their twenties in the early 1990s, a new crop of films emerged to capture their experience. *Reality Bites* (1994), directed by Ben Stiller, became a generational marker. The movie follows a group of friends as they navigate the challenges of early adulthood, from career struggles to romantic entanglements. Winona Ryder's character, an aspiring documentarian, embodies the creative, independent spirit of many Gen Xers.

Reality Bites also captured the "slacker" aesthetic that became associated with the generation. The term "slacker" was popularized by Richard Linklater's 1990 film of the same name, which followed a group of aimless 20-somethings in Austin, Texas. While the term was often used pejoratively, it also represented a rejection of the materialistic values of the 1980s and a desire for a more authentic, if uncertain, way of life.

Pulp Fiction and the Rise of Indie Film

The 1990s also saw the rise of independent cinema, with films such as Quentin Tarantino's *Pulp Fiction* (1994) breaking through to mainstream success. *Pulp Fiction*, with its nonlinear storytelling, pop culture references, and mix of humor and violence, was a sensation, grossing over $200 million worldwide.

Other indie films, like Kevin Smith's *Clerks* (1994), Richard Linklater's *Before Sunrise* (1995), and Doug Liman's *Swingers* (1996), captured the irreverent, dialogue-driven style that appealed to Gen X audiences. These films, often made on shoestring budgets, showed that you didn't need a major studio behind you to create something impactful and resonant.

The Lasting Impact

The films of Gen X's youth, from the Brat Pack classics to the indie breakthroughs, continue to shape popular culture. *The Breakfast Club* is still regularly referenced and parodied, its themes of teenage angst and self-discovery remaining evergreen. The independent film movement of the 1990s paved the way for the explosion of indie cinema in the 2000s and the rise of streaming platforms like Netflix and Amazon Prime.

Moreover, many of the actors and filmmakers who defined Gen X cinema are still major forces in the industry. Ben Stiller, Winona Ryder, Ethan Hawke, and Quentin Tarantino, to name a few, have had long and influential careers that continue to this day.

For businesses, understanding the films that shaped Gen X provides invaluable insight into the generation's values, humor, and aesthetic sensibilities. Whether it's the honest, slightly sarcastic tone of *Reality Bites*, the rebellious spirit of *Pulp Fiction*, or the nostalgic resonance of *The Breakfast Club*, the cinema of Gen X offers a rich vein of cultural touchstones to draw upon.

In the end, the films of Gen X's youth, like the music, aren't just entertainment; they're a reflection of a generation's hopes, fears, and desires. They offer a window into the experiences that shaped this influential group and continue to resonate as they move through middle age and beyond.

Core Cultural Moments—Divorce, Latchkey, and a Flannel Shirt

In view of the popular movies, it's consistent that Gen X pioneered a new model of slacker-chic cool, with the understated style of jeans, flannel shirts, and Doc Martens contrasting with the more materialistic 1980s. It's hard to say if art imitated life or vice versa, but the movie themes mentioned above played out in Gen X youth culture.

This is also the first generation of kids to experience a new social phenomenon: an escalated rate of divorce. Divorce rates skyrocketed in the 1980s during Gen X's childhood and teenage years. Divorce, of course, impacts the whole family and affected how Gen X kids felt about yet another institution: marriage. With a world view that includes divorce as a possible outcome in a relationship, Gen X delayed getting married more than earlier generations and were more likely to live together prior to tying the knot.[4]

"When I was in fifth grade and my parents got divorced, I was so embarrassed. I didn't know anyone with divorced parents. By the time I got to high school, so many of the kids were in the same boat as me. I didn't feel as much like a freak."

—GEN XER, AGE 53

This societal shift also gave rise to a broader view of single parenting and latchkey kids. The term *latchkey kid* refers to the Gen X kids coming home from school to an empty house while the parent was still at work. The Gen Xer latchkey kids were a perfect audience for the Sony PlayStation, which launched in 1995. It provided fun tech in a very entertaining format that was perfect for some home-alone downtime.

As youngsters, the Gen Xers were known as laid-back, alienated slackers in contrast to the Boomers. However, their vibe masked a resilient, independent streak born from the struggle to soldier on amid societal changes. It should be no surprise that this was the generation that spawned the grunge scene and the tech industry, two vastly influential cultural and economic forces.

Gen X—Talkin' 'bout My Education!

While Millennials are often portrayed as the most educated generation, Gen X actually holds that title. According to a 2017 Pew Research Study, 36% of Gen X women and 29% of Gen X men have a bachelor's degree. Overall, 32% of Gen X earned a bachelor's degree versus just 26% of Baby Boomers.[5]

Gen X Women: Educational Trailblazers

One of the most significant educational shifts for Gen X was the rise of women pursuing higher education. In 1982, when the oldest Gen Xers were in their late teens, women earned 49% of all bachelor's degrees. By 2000, when the youngest Gen Xers were in their early twenties, that figure had risen to 57%.

> "When I started my MBA program, only 15% to 20% of my class were women. I returned to my alma mater campus this spring to see that women were easily half of the student body. I never realized I was a trailblazer, but I guess I was."
>
> —FEMALE GEN XER, AGE 59

This trend continued into graduate education. In the 1980–1981 academic year, women earned 49% of master's degrees. By 2000–2001, that number had grown to 58%. This period also saw a significant increase in the number of women pursuing traditionally male-dominated fields such as law and medicine. Between 1980 and 2000, the percentage of law degrees earned by women rose from 30% to 47%, while the percentage of medical degrees earned by women increased from 29% to 46%.[6, 7]

The Ripple Effects

The educational achievements of Gen X women have had far-reaching impacts. Higher education has translated to increased workforce participation, with 76% of Gen X women employed, compared with 58% of Baby Boomer women at the same age.[8] It has also contributed to delayed marriage and childbearing, as well as lower fertility rates, as women focused on establishing their careers.

Moreover, the educational attainment of Gen X women has set the stage for the continued advancement of women in subsequent generations. Millennial women have continued to outpace men in college enrollment and completion, a trend that started with Gen X.[9]

The Economic Impact

The higher education levels of Gen X, and particularly Gen X women, have significant economic implications. College graduates earn 75% more than those with only a high school diploma, and those with advanced degrees earn even more. This increased earning power translates to greater consumer spending, as well as increased tax revenue and economic growth.

Furthermore, the fields that saw significant growth in female participation during the Gen X years, such as law and medicine, are among the highest-paying professions. As Gen X women have moved into leadership positions in these fields, they have not only increased their own economic clout but also paved the way for greater gender equality in the workplace.

Looking Forward

As Gen X moves through their peak earning years, their educational attainment will continue to shape their economic impact. Their high levels of education, particularly among women, have positioned them for leadership roles and high-paying careers. As they move into their 50s and 60s, they will also be better positioned for a financially secure retirement, thanks to their increased earning power.

In the end, the educational attainment of Gen X, particularly the strides made by women, is not simply a demographic footnote. It's a key factor in understanding the generation's values, lifestyle, and economic impact. As the first generation to see women achieve educational parity with men, Gen X has been at the forefront of a quiet revolution that continues to reshape the social and economic landscape.

All Grown Up Now

While the past helps set the scene and context for Gen X, to understand how this generation drives the economy, it is best to focus on them today. The statistics alone help frame the opportunity for businesses.

Gen X by the Numbers

Despite being a smaller cohort than Baby Boomers or Millennials, Gen X, with a population of about 65 million adults, wields significant economic clout.

- Gen X has $2.4 trillion in spending power.[10]

- Gen X has a median household income of $113,455, the highest of any generation.[11]

- 75% of Gen Xers own homes, also the highest of any generation.[12]

- 82% are married or partnered, and 71% have children under 18 in the home.[13]

- Gen X has an average net worth of $252,000, trailing only Baby Boomers.[14]

These stats paint a picture of a generation at the peak of its earning and spending power. With a high level of education, careers established, and families growing, Gen X drives key sectors from real estate to consumer goods. A 2022 CBRE survey found that Gen X now makes up the largest share of suburban home buyers.

> "Our bank sent an offer in the mail
> addressed to my 19-year-old son
> for a Gen Z credit card promo.
> First, he doesn't even look at the
> mail, and second, I'm the platinum
> card holder. Where's *my* deal?"
>
> —"INVISIBLE" GEN X DAD, AGE 49

Urban, Suburban, or Rural?

According to a 2018 study by the Pew Research Center, Gen Xers are almost evenly split between urban, suburban, and rural areas. The study found that 36% of Gen Xers live in suburban counties, 32% in urban counties, and 31% in rural counties.[15] This distribution is similar to that of the Baby Boomers but differs from Millennials, who are more likely to live in urban areas.

However, it's worth noting that these patterns can shift as generations age. Many Gen Xers who started their families in urban areas have moved to the suburbs for more space and better schools. In fact, a 2021 study by the National Association of Realtors found that Gen X makes up the largest share of suburban home buyers.

Homeownership and Family Life

Gen X has a high rate of homeownership, with 72% of Gen Xers owning their homes, according to a 2024 Redfin report.[16]

This is the highest rate among all generations, likely due to their stage of life and economic stability.

In terms of family life, 53% of Gen Xers are married, 8% are partnered, and over half have children under 18 in the home.[17] As the sandwich generation, many Gen Xers are also caring for aging parents while supporting their own children. We will explore this reality in a later chapter.

Consumption Habits Snapshot

Gen X, perhaps due to their life stage, financial responsibilities, and economic track record, are often known for their pragmatic approach to consumption. A report by American Express found that Gen X is more likely than other generations to seek out deals and discounts, with over two-thirds of its members saying they always look for ways to save money. However, the same report found that Gen X is more likely than other generations to prioritize spending on family, home, self, and health.

But don't be fooled into thinking they are limited buyers who are unwilling to spend on things that matter to them or that they are unsophisticated on how to leverage multiple buying channels.

Gen X has the highest brand loyalty of all generations, at 68%.[18] When asked why, Gen Xers reported it was because they use the brand regularly. Can it really be that easy to engage Gen X? Yep. One idea: Bring them on board with trial offers. If the product or service delivers value and it is something they want, then companies can expect repeat purchases and a high lifetime value. This pattern of consumption extends beyond simple household goods used daily. You might be surprised to learn this generation is the number one buyer and consignor of the high-end luxury brand Gucci. This generation is old enough to truly know what they want and confident enough to purchase despite what others think. Here is where pragmatism plays a strong role in accelerated consumption. Hooking Gen X can be a big win for any brand and is a high return strategy for loyalty programs.

Brand managers developing marketing programs should be aware that Gen Xers are as comfortable online as offline for their purchases and are fluid omnichannel shoppers. Their confidence in finding and buying brands online should not be surprising, as this is the first generation to pioneer e-commerce. Amazon was founded in 1994 and might be considered one of the largest shared experiences for this generation since most of its members were in their teens and early twenties when it started. E-commerce became an embedded purchasing behavior. As of May 2023, in the United States, Gen X represented the biggest consumer base of Amazon.[19] Gen X's online purchasing extends beyond the traditional e-comm websites; 51% of Gen Xers have purchased an item via social media, and over two-thirds report a positive experience.[20] These are digitally savvy consumers.

While Gen Xers trust e-commerce, they still shop brick-and-mortar. This buying behavior illustrates the need for companies to consider a multichannel experience to win the hearts and minds of these powerful consumers.

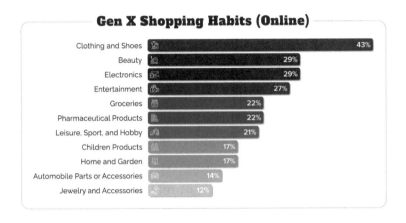

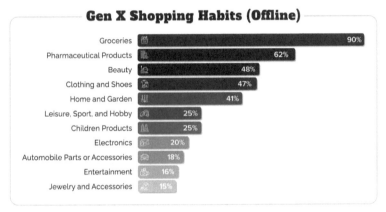

Data for both tables sourced from Klarna; reformatted for the book.

Conclusion—Putting It All Together

These current-day stats and insights help round out the picture of Gen X as a diverse, pragmatic, and well-funded generation. While they're split in terms of urban/suburban/rural living, they're united in their high rates of homeownership, views on education, approach to consumption, and their cultural backdrop.

Ultimately, Gen X's unique blend of characteristics—their technological savviness, their role as the sandwich generation, their high rates of homeownership and family focus—makes them a powerful and influential force in the US market. Understanding and catering to their needs and preferences will be increasingly important as they move through their peak earning and spending years.

They are the quiet drivers of massive economic trends, shaping sectors from housing to health care, education to entertainment. The sooner businesses recognize their unsung influence, the better positioned they will be to unlock new avenues of growth and connect with the most powerful spenders in America. It's no longer about *The Breakfast Club* and "Teen Spirit." It's about harnessing an economic powerhouse.

X FACTOR TAKEAWAYS
Understanding the Gen X Market

- **Significant Spending Power:** Gen X is a large cohort, weighing in at around 65 million adults and $2.4 trillion in annual spending. This is a market segment worth any business's attention.

- **Gen X Persona:** The cultural, economic, and social events that formed the collective psyche of Gen X have earned Gen Xers a reputation for being independent, cautious, and pragmatic. They have outgrown the laid-back slacker moniker.

- **Highly Educated and Successful:** Gen X boasts record high rates of education, 72% homeownership, and a median household income of $113,455—the highest of any generation.

- **Brand Loyal:** Gen Xers are prime consumers in practically all product and service categories, shopping both in stores and online. Gen X is the most brand-loyal generation.

CHAPTER 2

The OG Digital Natives

"Karma Chameleon"
—Culture Club (1983)

This chapter title alone is going to start a brawl, right? Well, *bring it.* Fully aware that the Millennials have been crowned the digital natives, we challenge that assumption. In this chapter, we highlight Gen Xers' historical digital role and then show why they matter today in our dynamic, technology-fueled society. Take note: there is a gap between the average Gen Xer's relationship with technology and that of Boomers, and grouping "everyone over 50" into the same bucket is a shortsighted mistake.

While Millennials and Gen Z often dominate discussions about digital consumption, Gen Xers have quietly become a formidable force in the digital landscape. "Chameleon" is the perfect metaphor: As ever-evolving tech comes and goes, they dependably adapt and adopt. Gen X's unique position as tech-savvy adults with significant purchasing power makes them a crucial demographic for marketers and brands to understand and target.

But before we explore today's landscape, let's go retro. Looking back provides some useful context on who has adapted to which technologies. We have already established that this generation is highly educated, and when it comes to tech, they have been lifelong drivers, adopters, and learners.

> **"Technology is only new if you remember what it was like before; otherwise, it is all you will ever know."**
>
> —JASON DORSEY, PRESIDENT, RESEARCHER & SPEAKER FOR GENERATIONAL KINETICS

Which Came First? The Internet or the Computer?

Gen X was there for all of it. As the earliest Gen Xers were entering college and the workforce, they were the ones moving from desk phones, voicemail, and mail rooms to desktop computers, email, and the internet. They pioneered the use of technology in both B2B and B2C, transforming *how* work gets done—and how we react as consumers. Their secret sauce? Gen Xers remembered what it was like before.

The Personal Computer Revolution

Gen X came of age during the personal computer revolution of the 1980s and '90s. A Pew study found this was the first generation to grow up with computers in their homes, with 55% reporting having used a computer by the time they were in high school.[1] As teenagers and young adults, they were among the first to use models such as the Commodore 64, the Apple II, and early IBM PCs.

In the workplace, personal computers became mainstream between 1985 and 1995. Initially, computers were often shared resources, with designated workstations used by multiple employees. Computers were steadily replacing electric typewriters on desks. By 1993, about 45% of workers used computers on the job, up from just 25% in 1984.[2] Gen X, entering the workforce during this period, was at the forefront of this transition.

Laptops weren't always the sleek silver beauties they are today, the kind ubiquitous at your local coffee shop. They started with some hefty 12-pound IBM models in 1986, which were even profiled in *Friends* season nine when Chandler gets a new laptop and calls out its weight!

"At my first office job, I remember helping my bosses log on to the new shared office IBM PC. It was a big deal, and everyone was really excited that it sent the documents directly to the printer. But you had to take turns and book time to use it, which caused its own workplace drama."

—GEN X ENGINEER, AGE 58

But the early models quickly evolved into the Gen X tool of choice. For college students, laptops started becoming more common in the mid-1990s. While not yet ubiquitous, they were increasingly seen on campuses. By 1998, about 30% of college students owned a laptop computer.[3] This trend accelerated rapidly, with Gen X being the first cohort to widely experience this shift. Some universities even began requiring laptop ownership for certain programs, particularly in business and engineering fields, starting between 1995 and 1997.

The laptop not only impacted education but the workplace as well. Even before universities mandated laptops, business use exploded. The pace of adoption, mainly driven by Gen X employees, was staggering. Laptop adoption surged in the late 1990s and early 2000s, becoming a defining force in how work was conducted. By 1999, the overall personal computer market had exceeded 100 million units annually, with laptops playing a growing role in this expansion.[4] Their portability and flexibility revolutionized workplaces, enabling employees to work beyond the office. This shift was cemented in the third quarter of 2008 when global laptop sales officially surpassed desktop sales for the first time.[5] Within a few years of their widespread adoption, laptops became integral across all organizational functions, paving the way for work to follow people home—a development that would fundamentally reshape work-life balance. But we'll delve into that topic later.

Internet Pioneers

Sorry, Millennials: not you. Gen Xers were the true internet pioneers.

They were the first to widely adopt the internet—referring to it as the *World Wide Web*—as a research information resource. And needless to say, they left the Boomers in their dust. Internet adoption rates among Gen Xers surpassed those of Baby Boomers by a significant margin in the late 1990s and early 2000s.[6]

Consider the atmospheric change in communications. The internet's takeover of the global communications landscape was rapid in historical terms. In 1993, it only communicated 1% of the information flowing through two-way telecommunications networks. By 2000, that figure had increased to 51%, and by 2007, more than 97%.[7] This was a Gen X-driven phenomenon.

The definition and accessibility of the internet quickly expanded its role as a repository of world data into new engagement models, industries, career paths, and more. Almost overnight, the need for a website, a domain, and a developer became commonplace vernacular. The rush to secure company website addresses began when the first .com domain was sold in 1985 and Netscape established SSL to make web browsing secure. Shockingly, the domain name industry generates around $9.5 billion in revenue.[8]

Business and revenue streams were transformed by the internet, a seismic shift spearheaded by Gen Xers—and they never looked back.

Workplace and Mobile Technology Adoption

The use of the internet gave rise to email, instant messaging, PowerPoint, social media platforms, and more. Tools we take for granted now were revolutionary, and in contrast to today's fast pace, they were slow at the time.

With its early dial-in beginnings, the universal internet soundtrack for Gen X was a cacophony of beeps, buzzes, screeches, and piercing tones while the modem attempted to connect. This was frequently followed by a greeting from early email provider AOL, whispering the siren song that elevated dopamine levels and spawned a Tom Hanks/Meg Ryan rom-com: "You've got mail." This new thing called email permeated our personal and work lives.

A Deloitte study found that Gen X workers were more likely than their Baby Boomer colleagues to embrace new workplace technologies—and not just email systems.[9] They also embraced project management software and early collaborative tools with verve and courage. Gen Xers were the ones who moved the business presentation from overhead transparencies to PowerPoint. (Google it, Millennials and Gen Z: it was a thing.)

While Millennials are often associated with smartphone culture, it was Gen Xers who laid the groundwork. They were the early adopters of cell phones, personal digital assistants (PDAs), and BlackBerry devices. In the mid-1990s, 2G, the first digital cellular phone system, emerged. It was piloted along with multiple brands of flip phones and mobile tech until Steve Jobs introduced the touchscreen smartphone in 2007. True to form, Gen Xers had higher smartphone adoption rates than Baby Boomers in the early years of the smartphone era.[10]

> **"I realized that I no longer had to listen to my desk phone voicemails at work. I just had to respond to the emails. It's the same requests, replies, sales pitches. They just changed devices."**
>
> —GEN XER, AGE 55

Working the Internet—Web 2.0

Remember that term? It referred to the second-generation World Wide Web characterized by increased user interactivity, B2B collaboration, and the rise of social media platforms. Web 2.0 gave rise to user-generated content, social networking, and cloud computing. On the business side, it gave rise to organizational tech, from marketing technology (martech) to sales tech to customer tech. It was the major shift that paved the way for today's applications and services.

In the early 2000s, the internet was all atwitter, even before X (originally known as Twitter) officially stole the spotlight. We saw the rollout of MySpace (2003), LinkedIn (2003), Facebook (2004), YouTube (2005), Reddit (2005), and of course, Twitter in 2006 and Tumbler in 2007—not to mention the absolute raft of bloggers. Internet and website design basically moved from static pages to ones "programmed for interactivity" and a focus on engagement.

Once there was an ocean of content populating Web 2.0, Gen X needed a tool to navigate it. While there were many early search tools, one in particular became the dominant resource: a little website called Google. Maybe you've heard of it? Google made its grand debut in 1998. If you don't think of Google as a Gen X tool, you should. The founders, Larry Page and Sergey Brin, are card-carrying Gen Xers, as were many of the early Google staff and user base. Google certainly became its own verb ("Google it") for consumers, but it also provided a huge B2B revenue trend for marketers and businesses buying search terms and adopting a pay-per-click model.

"It was 2004, and my big PR agency was explaining to me how mommy bloggers worked. People who did not know the bloggers followed them as if they were friends. I thought that was the dumbest thing I ever heard and wondered who had that kind of time to waste. Now I hire influencers by the truckload because it became the norm."

—GEN X MARKETER, AGE 57

At work, Gen X has been key for adopting and activating the avalanche of tech tools that have emerged. The rapid pace of expansion has required a level of flexibility that aligns well with this generation's strengths. For example, in martech (i.e., marketing technology), the number of tools has grown from 150 in 2011 to over 14,000 in 2024.[11]

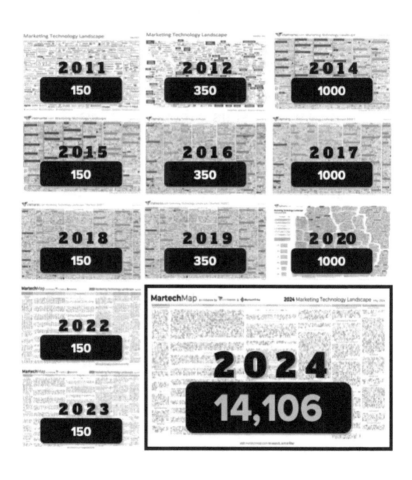

While Gen Xers are not responsible for *all* technology innovation, it is true that some of the most prominent names hail from this generation. Their technological fluency translated into digital entrepreneurship, boasting many pioneers of the dot-com era, business computing, and early social media platforms. Notable examples include the following individuals:

- Jeff Bezos (born 1964)—Amazon
- Michael Dell (born 1965)—Dell Technologies
- Marc Benioff (born 1964)—Salesforce
- Elon Musk (born 1971) —PayPal, Tesla, SpaceX
- Steve Chen (born 1978) and Chad Hurley (born 1977) —YouTube
- Jack Dorsey (born 1976)—Twitter, Square
- Reid Hoffman (born 1967)—LinkedIn
- Evan Williams (born 1972)—Blogger, Twitter, Medium
- Pierre Omidyar (born 1967)—eBay
- Marc Andreessen (born 1971)—Netscape Communications, Andreessen Horowitz

These Gen X entrepreneurs leveraged technology to create industry-disrupting companies. Their innovations have shaped the digital landscape we navigate today, from e-commerce and social media to electric vehicles and space exploration.

Don't Be Digitally Dismissive

While Millennials may have grown up in a more fully formed digital world, it was Gen Xers who actively shaped and molded that world. Their role as early adopters, digital pioneers, and ongoing learners challenges the notion that digital nativity is solely the domain of younger generations. Likewise, don't lump Gen Xers in with the Boomers. In general, their involvement and relationship with digital technology is markedly different from that of Baby Boomers. Gen Xers have been at the forefront of technological change, adapting to and embracing new digital tools throughout their lives. Unlike many Boomers, who had to learn digital skills later in life, Gen Xers grew up alongside evolving technology, making them more intuitive and comfortable with digital interfaces.

X-perts Weigh In

A few years ago, when studying Gen X for a work project, I tripped across an article on Medium titled "Gen X Will Not Go Quietly."[12] It waxed philosophic that most of Gen X is not dressing its age. That they grew up in the age of "flash and color, punk, metal, and hip-hop." That they learned to "live loud," and they weren't going to give it up with age. All of that resonated with me because I'm all of that. I'm Gen X.

The famously independent generation has been cited as the most skeptical. But also the most resourceful and adaptable. It's these qualities—along with the doors that opened with the introduction of computers and the internet into our lives—that have fueled this generation to be the *most* innovative, founding some 55% of startups. The generation with the *most* ideas, with the highest rate of patents filed. And the *most* entrepreneurial, with some 47% of small businesses founded and owned by them.

While Gen X isn't the digitally native generation that Millennials and Gen Z are, they are abundantly tech-savvy, with strong technical skills and a high capacity for generating ideas. Make no mistake, Gen Xers are the original digital pioneers.

So, to connect with them, meet them where they are. Feed their sense of independence. Inspire their entrepreneurial drive. And engage them as a community that isn't done inventing, starting, and progressing. Or, as Medium put it, a generational community that "will not go quietly."

—Lance Koenig
Chief Strategy Officer and Managing Partner
Rival

Gen X Today: The Underestimated Digital Powerhouse

Now that we have a clear view of this generation's tech IQ, let's dig into some areas where businesses can connect with these highly desirable buyers. The landscape is rife with opportunity; you just need a clear strategy and smart tactics to tap into the considerable purchasing power of Gen X.

Social Media Usage

Contrary to popular belief, Gen Xers are highly engaged on social media platforms. In fact, they outpace Millennials in weekly social media usage:

- Gen Xers spend an average of seven hours per week on social media, compared with Millennials' six hours.[13]

- 74% of Gen Xers are active on Facebook, making it their preferred social platform.

- Gen Xers make 55% more visits than other generations to social media sites.[14]

- 70% of Gen Xers report regularly watching videos on YouTube.[15]

This high engagement translates into significant marketing opportunities:

- 48% of Gen Xers follow brands on social media.[16]

- 71% are likely to purchase from a brand they follow on social media.

- 78% read reviews on social media before making purchases.

- Nearly 50% consider a brand's social media presence an important factor in their perception of the company.

These statistics highlight the importance of maintaining a strong, authentic social media presence to effectively reach and influence Gen X consumers and clients. While social media was once only thought of as a B2C vehicle, those days are long gone. Gen X follows influencers and subject matter experts for personal and professional reasons.

Video—Across All Channels for the Xers

From streaming video content to YouTube, mobile, websites, PLPs (product listing pages), product and service tutorials, and all social media, video is the preferred format. And Gen X consumes video content at a rate equal to or higher than other generations.

- Approximately 60% of Gen Xers stream movies weekly. (Deloitte's 2019 Digital Media Trends survey)

- 78% of Gen Xers watch online videos weekly, with 52% watching daily. (HubSpot, 2021)

- Gen Xers spend an average of 1.5 hours per day watching online videos. (Statista, 2022)

- 75% of Gen X viewers watch videos on their smartphones. (eMarketer, 2021)

- Gen Xers spend 1.5 times more time watching YouTube on mobile than Millennials do. (Google, 2020)

- 73% of Gen Xers watch videos on YouTube to learn how to do something. (Think Google, 2017)

- 44% of Gen Xers report viewing videos 1 to 4 times at work to learn about a company's product or services. (Brightcove, 2018)

- 65% of Gen X consumers have made a purchase after watching a brand's video on social media. (Animoto, 2020)

- 48% of Gen Xers prefer video ads over other types of online advertisements. (IAB, 2019)

- 78% of Gen X households subscribe to at least one streaming service. (Deloitte's 2021 Digital Media Trends survey)

- Gen Xers spend an average of 2 hours per day watching streaming content. (Nielsen, 2022)

- Gen Xers tend to prefer longer-form video content compared to those of younger generations, with an average preferred length of 2 to 5 minutes for informational videos. (Vidyard, 2021)

When crafting digital communication strategies targeting Gen X, incorporating video content should be a key consideration.

"I have so many streaming services now, but I still laugh when a new show I want to see announces that it's going to 'drop one new episode each week.' Um, isn't that what we used to call network TV?"

—EVERY GEN XER

The Brand Taking Advantage of Gen Xers' Social Media and Video Consumption

Jones Road, founded by makeup artist Bobbi Brown, has experienced significant success since its launch in October

2020. The brand, known for its clean beauty products, targets a broad demographic but has found a particular resonance with women over 50. This success can be attributed to the brand's focus on multipurpose, easy-to-use products that cater to the natural beauty and skin care needs of this age group.

Bobbi Brown created Jones Road to simplify beauty routines with high-quality, clean ingredients that appeal to women who prefer a minimalistic approach to makeup. The products are designed to work for all ages and skin tones, but the emphasis on natural "no-makeup makeup" looks and hydrating formulas makes them especially suitable for older women looking to enhance their natural beauty without heavy coverage.[17]

Jones Road has also benefited from a strategic marketing approach that leverages the Facebook and Instagram platforms, where women over 40 are highly active. The brand uses demo videos that show the product in use, with before-and-after shots. This demographic responds to video advertising, has significant purchasing power, and is keenly interested in products that promise both quality and simplicity. The brand's success with this segment is part of a broader trend where beauty brands targeting older women continue to rely heavily on social media for engagement and outreach.[18]

Internet Usage and Perceptions

It's important to note that Gen X's approach to the internet and being online differs significantly from that of younger generations. Consider the following statistics from WP Engine's 2019 research study:[19]

- A majority of Gen Xers, 59%, primarily use the internet for information, followed by entertainment.

- In contrast, 85% of Gen Zers associate the primary use of the internet with social media, then entertainment.

- According to a recent Nielsen study, just over 70% of Gen Xers are YouTube users, and how-to videos have the strongest draw due to their information-first orientation. In fact, 54% of Gen Xers on YouTube watch videos to learn how to do something. (Google/Ipsos, 2019)

This information-first mentality impacts how brands should communicate with Gen Xers:

- Prioritize value propositions and clear, informative content.

- Design messaging and cadence that reflects Gen Xers' preference for substantive information over purely entertainment-driven content.

Information vs. Entertainment

Question asked: Which aspects of the internet do you depend on daily?

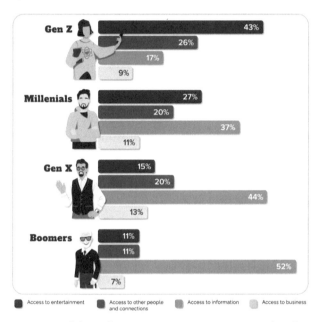

Stats sourced from the WP Engine report mentioned earlier.

Gen Xers' reliance on the internet is also noteworthy:

- Over 40% of Gen Xers report feeling uncomfortable without internet access for four hours.

- This compares to only 28% of Boomers, highlighting the significant digital divide between these adjacent generations.

Gen X demonstrates a surprising sophistication and expectation with new technologies that approximate that of younger generations:

- Over a third of Gen Xers, 36%, said they would prefer an internet that could predict and provide what they need at all times.

- This openness to predictive technology is close to Gen Z's 41%, indicating Gen X's willingness to embrace advanced digital solutions.

This receptiveness to new technology presents opportunities for brands to leverage predictive and personalized digital experiences to capture Gen X's attention and loyalty. This also runs counter to some assumptions about privacy concerns or resistance to being proactively "sold" the next logical solution.

Gen Xers Are Gamers. Surprised?

This trend goes back to that first Sony PlayStation, right? Today, 60% of Gen Xers report that they play video games.[20] They are also spending time on games ranging from Wordle to Block Blast. It might surprise you that nearly half of Gen Xers play video games at least once a week, and one-third subscribe to a gaming service—and yet, somehow, they still manage to get shit done.

Make no mistake: Gen Xers are playing, engaging, and purchasing within video game events. Consider the following chart from Deloitte's 2022 Digital Media Trends survey, which shows Gen X as the largest segment to make in-game purchases. This insight could impact the merchandise selection.

> "I've been playing video games forever, and I still love to unwind with *Grand Theft Auto*. I can also hang out with my daughter, who is super into *Minecraft*. Our big difference is, she can watch other people playing *Minecraft* on YouTube, and I just want to play."
>
> —GEN X DAD, AGE 49

The following chart shows the percentage of gamers spending money making purchases in a live in-game event.

	Total	Generation Z	Millenials	Generation X
Yes (Net)	82	64	88	92
Yes. I purchased digital merchandise	65	47	71	76
Yes. I purchased physical merchandise	34	27	39	35
No	18	36	12	8

Data sourced from Deloitte (Digital Media Trends, 16th edition, March 2022).

This population also enjoys game apps. Popular apps among Gen Xers typically include a mix of casual, puzzle, and strategy games, reflecting their preference for engaging and relaxing gameplay that can fit into their busy lives. Some of the top games that are widely enjoyed by this demographic include the following:

- Monopoly Go!: A digital adaptation of the classic board game, which has seen significant popularity across both iOS and Android platforms

- Wordle: A word game favorite that captivates players with its simple yet addictive letter play

- Words with Friends 2: A popular word game that combines the elements of Scrabble with social interaction, making it appealing for Gen Xers who enjoy word games and staying connected with friends

- Block Blast: A fun and addictive puzzle game that tests spatial reasoning skills by filling empty tiles with blocks of various shapes

- Subway Surfers: An endless runner game that remains a popular choice for its easy-to-learn but hard-to-master gameplay

These games are chosen not only for their entertainment value but also for their ability to provide quick, enjoyable sessions that fit into the busy schedules of Gen Xers. The combination of nostalgia, social interaction, and straight-forward gameplay makes these games especially appealing to this age group.[21]

The Rise of the Human-Digital Experience

So, what can we glean from the stats that helps us approach the OG digital natives in a way that resonates with them?

We know they value information and that this is what they first seek from digital interactions. We are aware that they embrace social media and consume video content on platforms such as YouTube at a rate equal to or greater than that of younger generations. We understand they appreciate predictive activations that can suggest for them what they would like or need.

Let's also not forget that this generation grew up with nondigital shopping and entertainment, so it's logical that they value direct interaction and personalized communication that characterize the "in real life" (IRL) experience. Their preference for personalized experiences is crucial for brand loyalty. They are open to advertising if it provides a value-add and is clearly relevant to them. The optimal approach is to blend one-on-one human communication with a best-in-class digital interface. We call this delivering a "**HUMAN-DIGITAL**" experience.

A Human-Digital experience offers the personalization that you would encounter walking into a well-run bar, café, or store where they truly know you. In a B2B setting, a Human-Digital experience would mirror the personal approach a sales rep or account manager provides to a long-term client. A Human-Digital experience for Gen Xers incorporates predictive personalization, informative communication, reasons to believe this product or service is right for them, and a frictionless experience that feels good—and is delivered digitally.

For great examples, look to Spotify and its curated, made-for-you mixes, recommendations, and "Discover Weekly" playlist based on one's listening history. Netflix, Max, and many other streaming services also try to assist users with future selections based on their personalized viewing history. Amazon may be the champion of using personalized algorithms to suggest exactly what shoppers may need next.

The Human-Digital experience also comes into play with direct-to-consumer (DTC) apparel retailers. The best ones take extra steps to gain consumer trust and add value. Rent the Runway, for example, shares the clothing size of the model pictured. They also allow outfit renters to post photos of themselves in the garment so there is a realistic expectation of how the purchaser may look in the garment. This specific content is a value-add and helps build brand loyalty.

In B2B and in our workplaces, we have seen a rise in account-based marketing delivering personalized content that makes buyers feel heard, along with "personalized" videos distributed via email. The technology that Salesforce and others have pioneered has enabled sales teams the world over to activate the next best action for clients based on data and behavior.

Other Human-Digital prompts include rating systems so the Gen Xer can see others' opinions of a product before committing. (More in future chapters about Gen X viewing life as a team sport!) A chat option is another useful feature, as is the ability to speak with a live person for more considered purchases or transactions. An additional spin on this idea might be pop-up notifications around holidays to advise shoppers on shipping dates (e.g., "You are sooo going to miss Valentine's

Day if you wait another day!"). This is a great way to turn love into guilt—and to ensure that box of chocolates arrives on time.

A digital interaction, especially in e-commerce, should mimic the experience of shopping at a neighborhood store with well-stocked shelves. At work, it is necessary to position the client as a hero for their company and career by providing personal, useful information and a frictionless, beautiful user experience. Now that's *amore*.

Here's a cheat sheet for creating a Gen X Human-Digital experience:

- **Prioritize Informative Content:** Focus on clear value propositions and substantive information in marketing and sales enablement materials.

- **Leverage Social Media:** Maintain an active, engaging presence on platforms such as Facebook and LinkedIn, where Gen Xers are highly active.

- **Emphasize Reviews and Social Proof:** Highlight customer reviews and testimonials, as Gen Xers heavily rely on these for purchasing decisions.

- **Embrace Video Content:** Develop engaging video content for both social media and streaming platforms to capture Gen Xers' attention.

- **Offer Personalized Experiences:** Leverage Gen Xers' openness to predictive technologies by providing personalized, data-driven experiences.

By recognizing Gen Xers' unique digital behaviors and preferences, brands can tailor their marketing strategies to effectively engage this powerful purchasing segment. As digital natives in their own right, Gen Xers represent a crucial bridge between older and younger generations, making them an invaluable target for businesses across various industries.

Gen X: The AI Adoption Accelerators

As we stand on the cusp of the AI revolution, Generation X is poised to play a crucial role in ushering in this new era of technology. Gen X's approach to AI is characterized by a balanced mix of caution and optimism. According to a Barna survey, while 35% of Gen Xers express skepticism about AI and 25% don't trust it, they are still far more likely than Baby Boomers to use this technology.[22] Gen X is already showing strong adoption of AI in the workplace. The 2023 Statista survey shows 28% of Gen X workers have adopted AI in their workplaces, slightly above Millennials at 27% and close to Gen Z at 29%.[23] This data suggests that Gen X is keeping pace with, and in some cases outpacing, younger generations in AI adoption.

This cautious yet practical approach is further evidenced by Gen X's more neutral stance on AI's future effects. A study found that 35% of Gen Xers were unsure whether AI would positively or negatively impact their work—a higher percentage than both Millennials and Boomers.[24] This open-minded uncertainty suggests a willingness to engage with AI and objectively assess its impact.

> "I'm not sure where AI will net out. No one really is. But it is here, and [my] learning how to use it will be essential for my job and my company."
>
> —GEN XER, AGE 45

Gen Xers' experience with technological evolution has prepared them for the AI revolution. More than half of Gen Xers agree that AI will change everyday lives; that's 15 percentage points higher than Boomers and nearly as high as Gen Zers.[25] This anticipation of change, coupled with their history of adapting to new technologies, positions Gen X workers as ideal guides for AI integration in the workplace.

Optimism, Skills, and Experience for AI's Integration

Despite their cautious approach, Gen X is notably more optimistic about AI's efficiency benefits than are younger generations. A recent study found that 89% of Gen Xers are optimistic about AI efficiency benefits, compared with only 72% of Gen Zers.[26] This optimism, combined with their practical approach, can help drive positive AI adoption in organizations.

Kevin Delaney, co-founder and CEO of Charter Works Inc., points out, "Older workers might be better equipped for working with AI, as the ability to delegate work and review what comes back are some of the most critical skills for applying AI tools effectively."[27] Gen Xers' experience in management and quality control positions them perfectly for this role.

Business Insider suggests that future jobs will likely involve less content generation and more quality control—a shift that plays to Gen Xers' strengths. Their institutional knowledge and professional experience make them ideal for providing the necessary supervision, judgment, and context that AI outputs require.

Accenture's recent generative AI report emphasizes that companies excelling in the AI era will be those that embrace reinvention. This requires redefining processes, reskilling people, and integrating a data and generative AI backbone into the digital core. As middle to upper management, Gen Xers are perfectly positioned to drive this organizational change.[28]

Conclusion

Gen Xers' unique combination of technological adaptability, professional experience, and balanced perspective on AI positions them as ideal catalysts for AI adoption in the workplace. Their ability to bridge the gap between traditional business practices and cutting-edge technology makes them valuable assets in the AI revolution.

As companies integrate AI into their operations, leveraging the skills, experience, and adaptability of Gen X employees can ensure a smoother transition into the AI-powered future. This generation can balance innovation with practical application and ethical considerations, guiding businesses through the transformative potential of AI.

Gen Xers' role as digital pioneers continues, much like their position at the forefront of the internet revolution. Their adaptive skills and historical perspective will likely play a crucial role in navigating the complex digital landscape of the future. As technology evolves, Gen X will continue to be the "Karma Chameleon" that knits the past, present, and future together, serving as both a key consumer segment embracing digital interactions and a critical element of the workforce ushering in the new technology revolution of AI.

X FACTOR TAKEAWAYS
Winning with the Gen X Digital Pioneers

- **Don't Be Digitally Dismissive:** Gen X is a tech pioneer, and its relationship with technology is much different from that of Boomers. Not all individuals over 50 years old are the same in terms of digital communication and creation.

- **Social Media Powerhouses:** Contrary to popular belief, Gen Xers are highly engaged on social media platforms, often outpacing Millennials in weekly usage. They are particularly active on Facebook and YouTube, presenting significant marketing opportunities.

- **Video Content Consumers:** Gen Xers demonstrate a strong preference for video content across various platforms, from streaming services to YouTube. They use video for entertainment, education, and the formulation of purchasing decisions, making it a crucial medium for reaching this demographic.

- **The Human-Digital Approach:** Personalized digital interaction leveraging, predictive tech, and authentic content are ways to engage this generation. Prioritize clear, informative content and value propositions.

- **AI Adoption Accelerators:** Gen Xers are well-positioned to lead AI integration in the workplace. Their balanced perspective, technological adaptability, and professional experience make them ideal catalysts for AI adoption, bridging the gap between traditional business practices and cutting-edge technology.

CHAPTER 3

Money Matters

"Money for Nothing"

—Dire Straits (1985)

M oney matters truly matter. The economy and access to money paint the backdrop of every generation's broader story, shaping our view of ourselves, our families, and our status in our communities. Often cited as the winner and loser of elections, the economy dictates whether the majority feel they're making enough money to survive or thrive and if they're earning their fair share. The Dire Straits song "Money for Nothing" is a perfect playlist selection as we explore this topic.

In this chapter, we'll explore significant market fluctuations, as well as the role money played for Gen Xers in their younger years and how it impacts their point of view, spending habits, investing patterns, and overall wealth building today. After all, "we got to move these refrigerators; we got to move these color TVs."

The Luckiest Martyrs?

Members of every generation tend to believe they had it the worst in terms of wages, income, luck, and the economy. We've all heard grandparents' stories of life's hardships from way back when. Members of the Silent Generation (born between 1928 and 1945) recount the lingering effects of the Great Depression and their coming-of-age experience after World War II as they helped build America. Older Boomers discuss the impact of Vietnam and their economy. Today, Gen Zers might argue that the value of a dollar makes college too expensive for the salaries they'll command afterward. The reality? Members of each generation endure a range of economic headwinds and tailwinds throughout their lives. This chapter looks at how these forces impact the amount of money Gen Xers managed to keep, save, and use.

Between 1990 and 2008, Gen Xers weathered two significant economic dips that affected their ability to earn, keep, and save: the dot-com era and the Great Recession. While these events didn't reach the epic proportions of the Great Depression, they certainly left their mark. Many Gen Xers were young enough to bounce back financially, but recovery took several years, undoubtedly shaping their views on money and wealth accumulation. This insight proves crucial for financial services companies and consumer brands targeting the lucrative Gen X cohort.

The Dot-Com Era

The last decade has seen intense focus on technology stocks. Since 2013, when CNBC business personality Jim Cramer coined the term FAANG stocks (Facebook, Amazon, Apple, Netflix, and Google), tech companies have dominated headlines as well as driven markets and investor returns. In 2024, FAANG further expanded into the Magnificent Seven (M7), including Alphabet, Amazon, Apple, Meta, Microsoft, Nvidia, and Tesla. Now we hold the seven up as role models in the stock market's laser focus on hot tech stocks.

It's easy to forget that an even more explosive technology cycle occurred back in the 1990s, with an even steeper trajectory and stock market speculation than today. Known as the "dot-com era" or the "dot-com bubble," this period marked a time of newfound innovation and the birth of new business models centered around the internet. This time frame coincided with the college graduation or early career years of Gen Xers.

Businesses seemed to spring up overnight, using the internet as their catalyst. In 1999, a staggering 39% of all venture capital investments flowed into internet companies. That year saw 457 initial public offerings (IPOs), mostly related to internet companies, followed by 91 in the first quarter of 2000 alone.

While consumer companies such as Amazon led the charge with new e-commerce, we also witnessed a massive uptick in B2B tech companies such as Cisco. Company valuations soared through the roof, employing new financial metrics that overlooked standard profitability measures. Private equity, venture capitalists, and mainstream investing fueled the rise. Think of it as a modern-day gold rush!

The dot-com fervor wasn't just a Wall Street phenomenon; it captured mainstream America's imagination. Pets.com and Monster.com introduced new business models for buying pet food online and searching for jobs. Prior to the establishment of these brands, the world mostly shopped at pet food stores for Fido's meals and mailed paper résumés to companies!

The dot-com era emphasized gaining market share through brand building and networking. For marketers, this era was a dream come true! It's been said that some start-ups allocated a whopping 90% of their budget to advertising.

The dot-com movement even commandeered the 2000 Super Bowl. With a TV viewing audience of 88.5 million people, Super Bowl XXXIV earned the moniker the Dot-Com Bowl. This game featured 14 advertisements from 14 different dot-com companies, each shelling out an average of $2.2 million per TV commercial. According to Wikipedia, of these trendsetting corporate advertisers, four remain active, five were acquired by other companies, and five are defunct or unknown.

> **"Seeing the ads on Super Bowl XXXIV changed the marketing landscape and made me switch my major in college. For the first time, we saw brand building as the lead revenue lever and a C-level discussion."**
>
> —GEN X CMO, AGE 46

This dynamic period ushered in new ways to build businesses, new go-to-market strategies, and a surge of enthusiasm for tech and the internet as the future. In hindsight, not all the new business models made sense or were sustainable. One example is Kozmo.com, which is mentioned in the documentary *The Rise and Fall of the Dot-Com Era*. Kozmo.com offered a revolutionary one-hour, on-demand delivery of small items, including DVDs, snacks, and books. However, it didn't charge delivery fees, which led to unsustainable business operations. In the film, it was reported that it couldn't keep up with its expenses and closed down in 2001 after burning through $250 million in investor capital. Remember, the concept of Amazon Prime didn't exist way back then, so maybe Kozmo. com was just ahead of its time.

In general, the dot-com era generated exciting business developments, but the unprecedented growth was followed by an unprecedented fall.

In the spring of 2000, the gold mines ran dry—and the dot-com bubble burst spectacularly. The precise event often cited as the beginning of the crash was the massive sell-off of technology stocks starting in March 2000. The Nasdaq Composite index, which had reached an all-time high of 5,048.62 on March 10, 2000, began a sharp decline thereafter. This decline continued over the following months, leading to a significant market downturn that affected many tech companies.

Several factors contributed to the bursting of the bubble, including overvaluation of dot-com companies, excessive speculation, and unsustainable business models. By October 2002, the Nasdaq had lost approximately 78% of its peak value.[1] Dot-com stocks had gone bust or teetered on the brink. Even blue-chip tech stocks such as Cisco, Oracle, and Intel saw their stock prices drop dramatically (it's reported they lost around 80% of their value.) The Nasdaq wouldn't return to its peak for 15 years, finally doing so on April 24, 2015.

The staggering details of the dot-com era profoundly impacted Gen Xers' psyches, bank accounts, and attitudes toward money.

The Dot-Com Era by the Numbers

- The dot-com bubble saw a rapid rise in US technology stock equity valuations fueled by investments in internet-based companies in the late 1990s.

- Equity markets grew exponentially during the dot-com bubble, with the Nasdaq rising from under 1,000 to more than 5,000 between 1995 and 2000.

- Equities entered a bear market after the bubble burst in 2001.

- The Nasdaq, which rose fivefold between 1995 and 2000, experienced an almost 77% drop, resulting in billions of dollars in losses.

- The bubble's burst caused numerous internet companies to go bust.

"I seriously thought I was going to be crazy rich. Like one of the stories I was reading about in the WSJ. I had stock options in the software company I worked for, and I thought I had it made. Until I didn't."

—GEN XER IN 2001

The Dot-Com Era and the Gen X Psyche

The roller-coaster ride had a dual impact on Gen Xers in terms of how they view finances and technology. Gen Xers who had started building their savings during the late 1990s took their first portfolio hit when the dot-com bubble burst. The significant losses Gen Xers witnessed in their stock investments—certainly a financial setback—may have fueled the "financial skepticism" persona we see in this generation today. Talk about bursting one's bubble!

The crash also ushered in a new era of more sustainable tech innovation. Many who were working in tech and counting on its ongoing positive trends were disappointed to see the "paper fortunes" of their company stock evaporate. As the dust settled, Gen Xers recognized the potential for long-term returns in technology investments, but with a crucial difference: they would now demand stronger business fundamentals and more realistic valuations.

This shift created a more stable tech market, and today, we see this generation confidently investing in diverse tech sectors, from established giants (FAANG, M7) to emerging fields such as AI and cryptocurrency. While the current AI investing boom might echo some dot-com era excitement, it's tempered by the hard-learned lessons of fiscal responsibility. The explosive, unsustainable valuations (at scale) of the dot-com bubble haven't returned. They have been replaced by a more measured approach to tech investment that balances innovation with sound business practices.

The Great Recession

The next big impact on Gen X was the Great Recession, which started in late 2007 and progressed into 2009. The statistics associated with this cycle are significant and dominated the markets, industries, and—quite literally—neighborhoods.[2]

The Great Recession Statistics

- Some 8.8 million jobs were lost.

- Unemployment spiked to 10% by October 2009.

- There were approximately 8 million home foreclosures.

- Close to $17 trillion in household wealth evaporated.

- Home prices declined by 40% on average.

- The S&P 500 declined by 38.5% in 2008.

- Between 2008 and 2009, $7.4 trillion in stock wealth was lost—an average of $66,200 per household.

- Employer-sponsored savings and retirement account balances declined by 25% or more in 2008.

The economic cycle of the Great Recession was the result of yet another bursting bubble: This time, it was the housing market. The culprit for this crisis? Subprime mortgages and subprime lending—two terms that can still make people wince.

Starting in 2001, successive decreases in the prime rate (the interest rate that banks charge their "prime," or low-risk, customers) had enabled banks to issue mortgage loans at lower interest rates to millions of customers who normally would not have qualified for them. This is what was referred to as subprime mortgage and subprime lending practice. As you can imagine, these "deals" incentivized buying a house and greatly increased the demand for new housing, which helped push home prices higher. This is fine when there is a low rate to secure. However, when interest rates finally began to climb in 2005, demand for housing, even among well-qualified borrowers, declined, causing home prices to fall.

Many home buyers were crushed financially. The movie *The Big Short* brought this nightmarish era to life in a recognizable (and star-studded) way. The film follows several groups of unconventional and quirky financial outsiders who realize that the US housing market is being propped up by risky and unstable subprime mortgages. While the big banks and mainstream investors are riding high, these outsiders predict the imminent crash of the housing market and financial system. It is well described as a complex dark comedy. Though not technically a Gen X movie, the film may offer the most complete and understandable explanation of the housing and mortgage crisis yet. It was certainly no laughing matter.

Being underwater with the asset that is typically your largest holding can be daunting. American households reportedly lost $16 trillion of net worth as housing prices fell by over 30%. Young households suffered the biggest loss. In 2005, the average Gen Xer was 25 to 40 years old and made up a significant portion of the first-time home buyers who had taken advantage of the easy access to loans. It is estimated that Gen Xers born in the 1980s lost the most wealth, measured as a percentage of what had been accumulated by earlier generations at similar age bands. Home may be where the heart is, but there were an awful lot of broken hearts.

This Gen X household group also took the longest time to recover, and some of them still had not fully recovered even 10 years after the end of the Great Recession. In 2010, the wealth of the median household headed by a person born in the 1980s was nearly 25% below what earlier generations of the same age group had accumulated; the shortfall increased to 41% in 2013 and remained at more than 34% as late as 2016.[3]

It is important to understand the psychological role the housing collapse of the Great Recession had on Gen X. In 2023, 38% of Gen X said buying a home was their greatest financial feat, according to a study by Empower.[4] How Gen X viewed borrowing money, mortgages in particular, and housing likely changed forever.

The Lost Generation Emerges

The Great Recession had a profound impact on Gen X, leading some economists to label it the "Lost Generation." This term reflects the significant financial setbacks Gen X faced in building and maintaining wealth during these key earning years. The time required to recover this lost wealth spanned nearly an entire generation (15 to 20 years), significantly impacting

Gen Xers' long-term financial growth. The big impacts were the following:

1. **Household Wealth:**

   Gen X experienced a substantial loss of household wealth, primarily due to the housing market collapse.

2. **Employment:**

   While the impact was mixed, it was still significant. About 72% of Gen Xers maintained employment and continued contributing to retirement plans. However, nearly 28% lost their jobs, a substantial portion of the generation.[5]

3. **Investments and Retirement Savings:**

   The stock market crash (57% decline between 2007 and 2009) severely affected Gen Xers' investments. 401(k) values plummeted, taking years to recover. In fact, it wasn't until 2013 that the S&P 500 regained its prerecession levels.[6]

4. **Long-Term Psychological Impact:**

   The recession replaced youthful optimism with financial caution. Many Gen Xers adopted a more pragmatic view of work, income, and retirement planning. Career advancement and bonuses were often slowed, altering their perspective on income stability and growth.

This combination of factors—lost wealth, employment instability, investment setbacks, and shifted financial outlooks—

contributed to Gen X's dubbed "lost" status. While not uniformly negative, these experiences significantly altered their financial trajectories and attitudes toward money, setting them apart from members of both preceding and succeeding generations. The new mantra with money became "preparedness for the unseen." Spoiler alert, read on: they still have plenty of capital today!

X-perts Weigh In

Speaking of Generation X tunes about money, remember that classic Barenaked Ladies song ending "If I had a million dollars, I'd be rich"? Sounds kind of whimsical nowadays.

This is the generation gripping a barbell of responsibilities for both the older and younger cohorts. Somehow, a million dollars doesn't look like enough to get the kids through college, contemplate parent eldercare, and be ready for retirement, let alone consider oneself "rich."

But no worries, because this is the "figure it out" generation. There's no pension anymore; latchkey kids manage their own 401(k)s. We beheld the rise and fall of the Pets.com sock puppet, so we're mostly not going to count on GameStop or any other meme windfall to bankroll us. We've seen life before and after the advent of the internet and smartphones, so we know we can invest online or hire an advisor to navigate our financial road map. And we've witnessed capital markets both create and destroy value on a large scale, so we are neither wholly jaded nor irrationally exuberant.

We approach investing with due respect. And alongside accumulated per capita wealth, that actually makes Gen X a pretty good target for the financial services industry and marketers in general. We don't expect anyone to do it for us, but we will avail ourselves of tools and experts. And we are open to an educated argument.

—Dana D'Auria
Co-Chief Investment Officer and
Group President, Envestnet Solutions
Envestnet, Inc.

The Pandemic and Money

The COVID-19 pandemic profoundly impacted all generations, reshaping lives for at least two years. However, from an economic perspective, Gen X was relatively less adversely affected. According to *Business Insider*, Gen X households, numbering approximately 34.6 million during the pandemic, experienced a $13 trillion increase in wealth.[7] This represents a 3.9% rise in the nation's total wealth.

Remember the housing challenges of the Great Recession? In contrast, the COVID-19 pandemic ushered in a new era of remote work, leading to the creation of Zoom-friendly home offices and enabling many to relocate due to the flexibility of working from anywhere. During this period, home prices soared. Gen X had already seen their home equity double from 2010 to 2018, and it rose even further during the pandemic.

Their financial assets also experienced a robust recovery. With more than double the income of older generations, Gen Xers were able to invest significantly more. Consequently, their equity assets grew to 10 times that of Millennials as the stock market rallied. According to data from the Federal Reserve, during the pandemic, household wealth distribution shifted from older generations to those who were reaching their peak earning years: our Gen X cohort.[8]

> **"I'd never want to live through it (COVID-19) again. But we survived. And financially, since we had our house at a low locked-in mortgage and a robust stock portfolio, we did not take the hit I anticipated."**
>
> —GEN X HOMEOWNER, AGE 52

Gen X and the American Dream

Money often dictates our ability to achieve our dreams and aspirations. For Gen Xers, having weathered various economic cycles and financial markets, the question arises: Do they feel positive or negative about their current and future status? In the United States, this sentiment is often encapsulated in the idea of the American Dream.

The American Dream is the belief that the United States is a land of opportunity for everyone, even for those who are financially insecure. It posits that hard work will lead to sufficient money to fulfill personal goals. But does this belief hold for Gen Xers after the economic and financial cycles they have experienced?

The reality of this dream is a question for all generations. Broad national data on economic mobility has already challenged the notion of equal opportunity in the United States, and the Gen X experience underscores these broader trends. Economists often ask, "Is this generation better off than the one before?" to gauge if the dream still exists, using factors like education, income, and net worth. On the surface, Gen Xers' cautious optimism seems to exist, with 56% believing the American Dream is alive. However, 69% believe it is tougher to obtain than in the past.[9]

According to the Pew Research Institute's 2018 study, Gen Xers are generally better off than their parents in terms of income, with the typical Gen X household earning about 38% more annually than their parents did at the same age. Some of this is due to women working more and pursuing higher education, etc. However, despite these income gains, many Gen Xers have accumulated less wealth, holding 27% less non-home wealth than their parents.[10] Meaning they make more money, but their overall wealth is less. This discrepancy is largely due to higher levels of debt, including mortgages, car loans, and education loans. Thus, while Gen Xers have seen increased earnings, they've faced challenges in wealth accumulation and economic mobility.

> "Sure, my husband and I together make more money than my folks did. But my mom never worked, and [my parents] did not have college loans. I would not trade my college degree or independence for anything, but we invested a lot to earn more."
>
> —GEN X DAUGHTER, AGE 48

While averages can provide a broad overview, they do not capture the entire picture of economic mobility and financial well-being for Generation X. It is certainly a tale of two Gen Xers, given the cycles they have been through, their education levels attained, and overall employment stability. Yes, according to the data, about three-quarters of Gen Xers have higher incomes than their parents, indicating they are financially better off in terms of earnings, but that leaves a quarter of them who do not earn more.[11] This highlights an opportunity for the financial industry to take notice of both segments and help some Gen Xers make up ground, as well as help others build more wealth.

Conclusion

It's fair to say that Gen Xers experienced a lot of economic challenges throughout their early working years. Whether it was living large through the dot-com bubble or feeling the long-term effects of the Great Recession, they have seen a lot. They have navigated fluctuating job markets, unexpected debt levels, and shifting technological landscapes that clearly have shaped their views on the relationship between money and financial stability.

However, despite the economic turbulence, Gen Xers are resilient. They moved through the years of uncertainty and, for the most part, emerged stronger. Their story is not just one of recovery but also one of adjustment, underscoring how Gen X has managed to persevere and redefine success. Don't be fooled by their pragmatic approach to money; it doesn't mean they aren't excited to be part of the next wealth-building innovation. In fact, they echo the sentiment of Dire Straits' "Money for Nothing." They've moved the refrigerators, they've moved the color TVs, and they're building their version of the American Dream. Time to quit calling them the Lost Generation. Gen X is just getting started!

X FACTOR TAKEAWAYS
Gen X Money Insights

- **They want to be prepared.** They are pragmatic about unforeseen cycles around the corner. Gen Xers firmly believe in an emergency fund and learn to live below their means.

- **It ain't over till it's over.** Gen Xers who came from middle-income families have a near equal likelihood of ending up in the top fifth or bottom fifth income distribution—meaning equal promise and peril. Gen X can be approached from the positive "keep moving forward" mentality.

- **Investing is the way to future money.** Surprisingly, the dot-com era did not throw Gen Xers off the belief that technology companies and stocks are the path to future money. This is likely because they lived through the rebound and saw the massive global impact tech has enjoyed.

- **They're adaptable, with a healthy level of skepticism.** While they see the long-term value of money, they can be skeptical. This group experienced the general elimination of pensions, which were replaced by self-opt-in 401(k) plans. Gen Xers still feel housing is the largest financial achievement but have adapted to the reality that it can't be the only place to invest their money.

CHAPTER 4

The Sandwich Generation

"Take On Me"

—A-ha (1985)

Picture this: a Gen Xer juggling a video call with their aging parent's doctor while simultaneously helping their teenager with college applications and sneaking glances at their own retirement account. This isn't just multitasking; it's the daily reality for millions of Gen Xers who find themselves squarely in the middle of the sandwich generation.

The term *sandwich generation* was coined by social workers Dorothy Miller and Elaine Brody in 1981, and in the years since, it's Gen X who has truly come to embody this role. As much as Gen X is financially established, it is also a sandwich generation, supporting both Millennial and Gen Z children, as well as elderly Boomer and Silent Generation parents. A report by the National Endowment for Financial Education found that a remarkable 34% of Gen Xers are financially supporting parents, and 23% are supporting adult children.[1]

This dynamic gives Gen X an outsized influence on the spending of other generations. Whether it's cosigning their kids' first lease or paying for their parents' prescriptions, Gen Xers often control or supplement the purse strings for an entire extended family. With both their parents and their kids needing Gen Xers to financially "Take On Me," businesses that cater to the modern multigenerational reality will succeed.

The Triple Play: Parents, Children, and Self

Gen X's sandwich generation status creates a triple play of responsibilities and economic influence: caring for aging Boomer parents, managing their own needs and wants, and supporting their children (often Millennials and Gen Zers). Each of these roles comes with its own set of financial implications and market considerations. Let's break them down:

Caring for Aging Boomer Parents

As the Baby Boomer generation ages, Gen Xers are increasingly taking on caregiving responsibilities for their families. Studies show that 40% of caregivers are between 45 and 64 years old, squarely in Gen X territory.[2]

- Financial Impact: Not everyone's Boomer parents are financially prepared for the long haul. From assisted living to home modifications, prescriptions, and daily living expenses, costs can be astronomically high, and Gen X kids frequently have to assist their parents with these expenses.

- Time Investment: Caregivers spend an average of 24 hours per week providing care. This calculation is based only on physical care and does not include the hours of working to understand health-care billing, insurance, and all the legal and logistical paperwork.

- Mental Impact: Dealing with a parent's affairs and striking the balance of delivering the help and respect that the parent requires is an emotionally demanding task. Dr. Atul Gawande's *Being Mortal* is a great book to lend perspective on that journey.

The Financial Impact of Senior Living

As Boomer parents age, many Gen Xers face the daunting task of navigating senior living options. Many seniors elect to stay in their homes for as long as possible, but this is not a viable option for all. While senior living options offer many benefits to the older parents and the adult children, the financial burden can be staggering:[3]

- According to Genworth, the median annual cost for assisted living in the United States is $64,200.

- For nursing home care, the median annual cost jumps to $104,028 for a semiprivate room and $116,800 for a private room.

- Genworth's survey shows average in-home care that ranges from $5,700 to $6,292 per month, depending on the location and the level of care needed.

Let those figures sink in for a minute and then couple them with the reality of longer life expectancy. With these costs, it's not surprising that the sandwich generation's needs are reshaping the housing market. A 2023 study by John Burns Real Estate Consulting found that 41% of Americans buying a home are considering accommodating an elderly parent (or adult child).[4]

As Boomers aim to age in place, there is a range of home modification products to make helpful accommodations. Gen X is often responsible for installing, coordinating, and financing these home modifications. This creates opportunities in the construction and home improvement sectors if businesses know how to reach the Gen X consumer and not just the aging parent. In addition to traditional home modifications, there's a range of new age tech that facilitates seniors living at home longer. From telemedicine platforms to home health monitoring devices, Gen X is a prime market for products that can help its members care for their parents remotely.

In fact, the sandwich generation's pain points might be the catalyst for the rapidly expanding age tech category. According to the USC Leonard Davis School of Gerontology's 2023 Aging is the Future Entrepreneurship Symposium, age tech stands at $1 trillion and is on track to hit $2 trillion. The technology encompasses a wide variety of solutions, including smart appliances, connected home devices, wearable robotics, and e-learning platforms. Gen Xers are at the forefront of adopting tech to help their parents, as well as themselves, in the coming years. Not surprisingly, Gen Xers are spearheading many of the start-ups in this area. Given their appreciation of new business models during the dot-com era, this might be a place where we see Gen Xers take charge of innovations and investing.

> **"I never thought I'd be researching walk-in tubs and stair lifts in my 40s, but here we are. It's like I'm furnishing two houses—mine and my parents'."**
>
> —GEN X DAUGHTER, AGE 47

Today, Medicare and Medicaid pay for two-thirds of senior care, but it is up to the families to provide the balance. The costs vary greatly depending on geography and required care level. Genworth's website is a helpful starting point for personalized research on median costs. Whether it's financing a senior living solution or funding in-home help and tech adaptations, the potential for economic stress has increased for Gen Xers as their parents outlive their original financial plans.

Time Investment

It's not just an issue of money. For Gen Xers caught in the sandwich generation squeeze, there is a time challenge as well. The caregiving journey often comes with complex accounting and legal responsibilities. Gen Xers frequently find themselves navigating unfamiliar territory with Medicare, Medicaid, supplementary insurance plans, and legal needs. Sounds like fun, right? Managing the paperwork can feel like a second job, and service providers who figure out how to help Gen Xers navigate the bureaucracy will be the winners. Some of the key "need-to-knows" for Gen Xers include the following:

1. Power of Attorney (POA): This legal document allows a designated person to make financial decisions on behalf of an aging parent. Gen Xers often take on the role of POA, managing everything from bill payments to investment decisions. It's best to have this document in place years before they are needed.

2. Health-care Proxy: Similar to a financial POA, this document designates someone to make medical decisions if the parent becomes incapacitated. Like the POA, having this arranged well in advance is ideal.

3. Advanced Directives: These documents outline a parent's wishes for end-of-life care, often requiring difficult conversations between Gen X children and their parents.

4. Guardianship: In some cases, Gen Xers may need to pursue legal guardianship to make decisions on behalf of a parent who is no longer capable of doing so for him- or herself.

"I spent weeks trying to understand the difference between a springing power of attorney and a durable one. It felt like I was back in school, only this time the stakes were much higher."

—GEN X MARKETING EXECUTIVE, AGE 45

Several Gen Xers we interviewed talked about their experiences when an older parent passed away unexpectedly and without legal paperwork, trusts, and wills in order. Almost all of them expressed a version of the same sentiment: "I found a legal service to help me with my own affairs so my kids never have to go through this mess." Getting family law paperwork in order is such an easy thing to put off, but as Gen Xers become the family glue, it's work that must get done.

Time commitment will also vary for Gen X kids depending on their proximity to their parents. The children who live the closest tend to experience a double-edged sword: more quality time with their parents but also full responsibility for local errands and health-care coordination. Depending on a parent's health, these demands can become so overwhelming that it becomes difficult to impossible to simultaneously manage a full-time job. And to state the obvious, Gen X's role in health-care decision-making is twofold: for their parents and themselves.

> **"I'm coordinating doctors' appointments and medications for my dad while also trying to stay on top of my own health screenings. It's like being an air traffic controller but for health care."**
>
> —GEN X SON, AGE 48

The out-of-town children have a different type of time management challenge. They need to find stretches of time to fly or drive to their parents and try to stay connected with the "situation on the ground." These children often provide their local siblings with a much-needed break from the responsibilities of caregiving. Remotely located children usually try to contribute to the situation by managing paperwork through online channels. This is becoming a more common way to divvy up generational care management. Companies that employ a Human-Digital approach to streamline the digital management will be rewarded with Gen Xers' loyalty.

The Emotional Toll

Beyond the financial and time management challenges, the emotional burden on Gen X caregivers is immense. Many find themselves in a role reversal, parenting their own parents while still raising children.

This constant juggling act takes a toll on Gen Xers' mental health and relationships. A recent study by the National Alliance for Caregiving found that 40% of caregivers report high emotional stress as a result of their role.[5] Coping with a parent's aging, especially if it involves their failing health, is difficult, to say the least.

Helping Gen X with the Parent Trap

For businesses attuned to these challenges, the Gen X caregiver market presents significant opportunities. Financial planners, insurance brokers, legal services, pharmaceutical companies, health-care providers, home remodelers, and age tech providers are just a few of the business categories that have the opportunity to deliver gold star client service and drive customer loyalty. A few of the biggest opportunities include the following:

- Financial Products: Specialized banking accounts, insurance products, insurance counseling, and investment vehicles designed for multigenerational financial planning fill a key need.

- Legal Services: Simplified estate planning tools, online legal document preparation, and specialized elder law services help the sandwich generation navigate legal waters.

- Time-Saving Products and Services: With responsibilities pulling them in multiple directions, Gen X caregivers value products and services that save time. Meal delivery services, housekeeping services, and time management apps are particularly appealing.

- Flexible Work Arrangements: The same National Alliance for Caregiving study mentioned earlier reported that 61% of caregivers have had to make workplace accommodations due to caregiving. Companies offering flexible work arrangements are more likely to attract and retain Gen X talent.

- Mental Health Support: The demands of caregiving take a toll. A study in the *Journal of Applied Gerontology* found that sandwich generation caregivers report higher levels of stress than other caregivers. This creates a market for stress reduction products, mental health services, and self-care offerings.

- Technology Solutions: Gen X caregivers are tech-savvy and open to solutions that can help them manage their responsibilities. From care coordination and medication management apps to remote monitoring devices, there's a growing market for caregiving technology.

As Gen Xers continue to navigate these complex waters to help their parents, businesses that can offer solutions to ease their burden—whether financial, legal, or emotional—stand to gain loyal customers and a significant market share.

X-perts Weigh In

As Gen Xers step into caregiving roles, many of us are discovering that caring for aging parents involves both technology and patience. One key lesson is that while tech can support us, it doesn't replace the importance of understanding our parents' readiness to accept help. Often, we want to solve problems quickly, but it's crucial to recognize that meaningful care happens when we meet them where they are—on their terms.

Gen X is well positioned to integrate advanced technology into caregiving, having adapted to everything from mobile phones and the internet to social media and AI. Still, technology is only a tool. At its core, caregiving remains about preserving dignity, fostering independence, and ensuring our parents feel supported.

Innovative solutions, like smart home systems, bring valuable assistance by addressing safety and providing new ways to communicate issues. These systems can reduce the strain on caregivers by offering real-time insights, allowing families to stay connected even from a distance. Yet, while this technology can provide added peace of mind, it's still the emotional and human connection that ensures both generations can thrive.

—Cathy Minter
Co-founder and CEO
and
Dawn Newsome
Co-founder, President, and CTO
Wisdom.io

Gen X Child Support

It's not just the parents; it's also the kids. Many Gen Xers are parents to Millennials and Gen Zers, and as recent studies reveal, they are often supporting them well into adulthood. This extended financial support is reshaping traditional notions of financial independence. But parents have always helped their kids out to some extent, so what is so different about today's landscape for Gen Xers and their kids?

The financial landscape facing Millennials and Gen Zers is markedly different from what Gen Xers experienced, largely due to several interrelated economic factors. The average cost of college tuition has increased by 25% in the last 10 years.[6] This sharp increase in education costs has led to a corresponding rise in student loan debt. The Federal Reserve reports that as of 2021, the total US student loan debt exceeded $1.7 trillion, a figure that has more than tripled since 2006.[7] Housing costs have also surged, with median home prices increasing by over 28% between 2019 and 2021 alone.[8] Meanwhile, wage growth has not kept pace with these rising costs. The Pew Research Center found that the average hourly wage, when adjusted for inflation, has roughly the same purchasing power it did 40 years ago.[9] This combination of factors—skyrocketing education and housing costs, massive student loan debt, and stagnant real wages—has created a perfect storm of financial challenges for younger generations, often necessitating continued financial support from their Gen X parents.

Tuition

Saving for college really has taken on a whole new dimension for Gen Xers and their kids. In 2024, the average in-state public four-year institution is $27,146 per year. Out-of-state students pay on average $45,708 per year, and private university students pay an average of $58,628.[10] As Gen Xers value education, they are focused on funding as much as they can and getting valuable information about scholarships, loans, and other tools to bring down the college sticker price.

TikTok Made Me Buy It

But college is not the only rising price tag. The Gen Xers with tweens and high schoolers are footing the bill for an ever-expanding range of family streaming services and mobile phone plans. The trick is, once they are on the "family plan," they never seem to move off. The DoorDash and Uber bills also seem to roll up to Mom's credit card, as do some of the TikTok-featured beauty and skin-care products that are being targeted to a tween audience. The instant availability of e-commerce on social media has made it challenging for parents to instill budgeting and sound financial planning in their kids. And while some of the Gen Zers have managed, others are struggling with credit card debt and heading back to TikTok for financial advice (see "loud budgeting" on TikTok). But let's give these kids a break. Related to Chapter 1's discussion of the importance of music to a generation, the prices of concerts today have skyrocketed. Even if we remove Taylor Swift's Eras Tour from the equation, seeing live music is a budget buster for most younger Gen Zers. It's part of a growing list of expenses that once came from a teenager's spending money but have now shifted to Gen X parents. Concert tickets can easily cost $400 each, and attending live theater events can be just as expensive in large metros.

Cars, Weddings, and Rent

Having kids is a joy, so this chapter is not meant to be a buzzkill, but there are three words that impact the sandwich situation and how to think about the Gen Xers' situation: Cars. Weddings. Rent. Even crappy, old used cars became pricey. It's a real expense for the Gen X parent and Gen Z child to navigate. Next up: weddings. The Knot and Zola report that the average cost of a wedding in the United States in 2023 was around $35,000, which represents a $5,000 increase from the previous year.[11] Weddings are supposed to be happy milestones and memorable events for families. While they do seem to be taking place later in life for Millennials and Gen Zers, the expense involved is not just the wedding itself. Somehow, these weddings have grown into multi-event spectaculars that involve the wedding party flying to exciting locations for bridal showers, bachelorette parties, and engagement parties. For the bridal party, coordinated theme dressing has become part of the social deal. Like a sorority rush party that just won't quit, these wedding traditions are getting very expensive for the young people participating in the event. It's just one of the contributors to the Gen Z budgeting dilemma and the Gen X bailout machine.

Rent. This is a biggie. From the time when Gen Xers graduated and moved out on their own, rising rent has been more than an inconvenient expense; it has become a force behind a cultural change. Across the country, entry-level housing prices and rents have risen, making it hard for young graduates to afford housing. This means that it has become much more common for adult kids to move home with their parents to save money before moving into a place of their own. This will be an interesting trend to watch and see how it impacts Gen Xers' spending.

> **"I thought I'd be an empty nester by now, but my 25-year-old is back home, 'figuring things out.' I love having her around, but it definitely impacts our budget and retirement planning."**
>
> —GEN X MOM, AGE 50

Again, so what's the big deal? We love our kids and want to spend money on them. The big deal is that the unplanned cash outflows during Gen Xers' prime earning years take away from their ability to accumulate wealth. And that behavior can trip up future plans.

Balancing Their Own Needs and Wants

While juggling responsibilities for others, Gen Xers are also in their prime earning and spending years. They're at the peak of their careers—around 53% of leadership roles are held by Gen X (more on that in Chapter 6)— and they have significant purchasing power (holding an estimated $2.4 trillion in spending power, as noted in Chapter 1). On top of this, GenX is poised to inherit wealth from the older generation, as referenced in Chapter 3.

This apparent disposable income creates opportunities across various sectors, such as luxury goods and travel. With established careers, Gen X is a key market for high-end products, experiential travel, and the fabled "bucket list" items.

We are going to dive a little deeper into the Gen X "It's My Time" spending list in Chapter 9. However, when it comes to discussing the sandwich generation, the focus is really on recognizing how Gen Xers balance investing in their future and indulging themselves ("Haven't I *earned* that Porsche?") with supporting family members—both older and younger.

> **"I'm trying to save for retirement, save for my kids' college, and help my parents with their medical bills. I need an advisor who can help me juggle all of this."**
>
> —GEN X PROFESSIONAL, AGE 52

Given their life stage, Gen Xers require guidance to prioritize their financial needs, if possible. When Gen Xers find themselves part of the sandwich generation, taking care of both their children and their aging parents, it can derail retirement plans. A total of 33% of sandwich caregivers have sacrificed long-term savings to support their family members.[12]

Using long-term savings for day-to-day expenses presents a daunting future depending on the amount of time Gen Xers might be in this situation. To illustrate the situation, here are some additional statistics to frame the impact.

- A total of 35% of sandwich generation adults support their parents financially, spending around $725 each month, which amounts to between 13% and 16% of their household income.

- Those financially supporting their adult children estimate that they spend an average of $567 per month on doing so, which accounts for 6% to 8% of their household income.

The amount of household income going to the sandwich generation's needs can conservatively amount to more than $15,000 a year. If the Gen Xer could instead invest that $15,000 each year and earn just a 5.5% return for 10 years, they would have an additional $200,000 in their wealth bucket. The financial hardship of landing in the sandwich generation is clear. It's no wonder that 61% of them are concerned about the future, and 50% worry about being able to continue to juggle supporting their parents and their children.

"Clients only have a certain amount of money to devote to their financial goals, and right now, Gen X is probably juggling more big-dollar goals than other generations. Helping clients understand how they are tracking toward their various goals can help prioritize where funds should be directed."

—JEFF BURKE, FOUNDER OF 7TH STREET FINANCIAL

Jeff Burke, the founder of 7th Street Financial and a Gen Xer himself, has advised many clients facing this struggle. The first step, he says, is to give them a clear picture of where they stand with all these competing objectives—and then help with the balancing act.

The Future Economics of the Sandwich Generation

As Gen Xers age, their sandwich generation status will evolve. In the coming years, we can expect several emotional and economic changes to impact them. The financial squeeze with their kids may be more short-term and manageable. As their Millennial and Gen Z children become more established in their careers, the nature of financial support may change, potentially freeing up resources for their own Gen X needs.

In contrast, the aging parent slice of the sandwich may result in ongoing stress and responsibility. The ongoing evolution and shift in caregiving stages is daunting. As their parents age, Gen Xers may shift from a supportive role to a primary caregiver role, potentially impacting their careers and financial situations. Additionally, as they expand their role as caregivers, there is an increased focus on their own physical aging and financial urgency. This will likely drive increased interest in preventative health care and long-term care planning.

Lastly, we may be on the verge of Gen Xers driving an exploding age tech industry, fueled by them as entrepreneurs and certainly as adopters. Gen Xers are likely to continue embracing technology solutions to manage their multiple responsibilities, driving innovation in areas such as health-care tech and financial planning tools.

> **"I've become a pro at finding apps and gadgets that help me keep track of everything. If it can save me time or give me peace of mind, I'm willing to invest in it."**
>
> —GEN X CAREGIVER, AGE 54

Conclusion

Gen Xers' position in the sandwich generation is more than just a demographic curiosity; it's also a major economic force. Their triple role as caregivers to aging parents, providers for their children, and consumers in their own right makes them a crucial target market across multiple industries.

For businesses, understanding and catering to the unique needs of this sandwich generation presents significant opportunities. From health care and financial services to technology and housing, companies that can offer solutions to help Gen Xers navigate their complex responsibilities stand to gain loyal customers and substantial market share.

As we move forward, the influence of Gen Xers as members of the sandwich generation will persist. While we've discussed their Millennial and Gen Z kids, we can't ignore that many of the younger Gen Xers also have Gen Alpha kids. So that "payroll" obligation is not a short-term expense. Gen Xers' economic power, combined with their pivotal family role, positions them as key decision-makers and consumers for years to come.

As Gen Xers' parents and children require them to "Take On Me," they will need financial, professional, and technological help to make it work. Businesses that recognize and respond to the needs of this generation will be well-positioned to thrive in the evolving economic landscape.

X FACTOR TAKEAWAYS

Gen X Sandwich Generation Insights

- **Financial Squeeze:** Gen Xers are experiencing significant financial pressure from multiple directions, supporting both aging parents and adult children while trying to manage their own financial needs and retirement planning. This "sandwich" situation has a major impact on their spending patterns and financial decisions.

- **Caregiving Responsibilities:** Gen Xers are increasingly taking on caregiving roles for their aging parents, which involve not just financial support but also emotional and time investment. This impacts their work-life balance and creates a market for caregiving support services and technologies.

- **Extended Support for Adult Children:** Due to economic factors, including rising education costs, housing prices, and stagnant wages, Gen X parents are often financially supporting their adult children well into adulthood, affecting their own financial planning.

- **Technological Adoption:** Gen Xers are embracing technology solutions to manage their multiple responsibilities, driving innovation in areas such as health-care tech, financial planning tools, and age tech products. This presents significant opportunities for businesses in these sectors.

- **Marketing Opportunities:** Understanding Gen Xers' sandwich generation status is crucial for effective marketing. Businesses that can offer solutions to help Gen Xers navigate their complex responsibilities—from financial services to time-saving products—have the potential to build relationships as well as gain loyal customers and substantial market share.

PART 2

Tapping Into the X Factor: The Super Categories and Winning Strategies

CHAPTER 5

The Midlife Categories That Count

"Livin' on a Prayer"

—Bon Jovi (1986)

"Whoa . . . We're halfway there"

W e are halfway there—halfway through this book. And statistically speaking, Gen Xers are about halfway through their average life expectancy. To use a Gen X phrase from the 1993 movie *Menace II Society,* "Shit just got real." For this population, it's time to take stock, make moves to secure their futures, commit to what is most important, and enjoy the present.

We've touched on several factors that have shaped Gen Xers' psyches, obligations, and bank accounts. In the following chapters, we are going to look at the future and the "So, what now?" question. Whether you are a Gen X reader gauging where you fit in or a business looking to leverage this underserved customer segment, the following chapters serve as a guide to products, services, work structures, and philosophies that will be meaningful to this cohort over the next two decades.

There are three super categories that will be increasingly important to Gen X in the foreseeable future. We call them the Three *W*'s: **WORK, WEALTH, and WELLNESS.** They sound logical enough, and exploring each category will reveal important nuances.

- Why Work:
  - o Today, Gen X represents approximately 31% of the US workforce, and it's estimated that the percentage of over 50-year-old workers will drastically increase over the next decade.[1] Over 53% of the Fortune 500 CEO positions are held by Gen Xers. The impact of

this generation on companies and industries can't be underestimated but is often overlooked. Additionally, figuring out how to motivate and use Gen X will be a catalyst for future generations as they age.

- Why Wealth:
  - o Gen X controls over $48 trillion in assets, making it *the* target segment for financial services, insurance programs, retirement solutions, and wealth-building options.[2] Gen Xers are in their peak earning years and eager to have professional help with their money and wealth. The financial services industry and wealth management have a unique opportunity to adapt programs and communications that supercharge Gen X to invest for years to come.

- Why Wellness:
  - o Many Gen Xers value personal wellness, having grown up during the rise of fitness culture and increased health awareness. Did we mention they are between 45 and 60 years old at the time of this book's publication? Staying healthy now takes some effort. Gen Xers also pioneered work-life balance and are unwilling to sacrifice, so wellness extends beyond diet and exercise to encompass mental well-being and more. Gen Xers have the disposable income to purchase wellness products and services, so brands who target them directly are playing to win.

We'll also touch on how to connect with Gen X through creative messaging, media channels, and overall go-to-market strategies. In an informal 2024 study, we interviewed over 45 creative directors, marketing strategists, chief marketing officers, and chief customer officers from large and medium-sized agencies and brands. We asked them all the same question: When was the last time you received a creative brief or marketing request that focused on reaching Gen X? The only answers were: 1. Never and 2. It's been so long, I can't even remember. There is an opportunity to be had.

CHAPTER 6

Work

"Manic Monday"
—Bangles (1985)

I magine you're a Gen Xer, now 50 years old, who started working at age 20. Over that time, you've likely worked around 48 weeks a year, totaling approximately 1,440 weeks on the job. That's about 57,600 logged-in hours. That's a whole lot of manic Mondays.

Sure, Millennials may have coined the term *the Sunday scaries,* but Gen Xers have been powering through them for more than 25 years. These numbers highlight the dedication and effort that the average Gen Xer has invested in their work life, contributing not just hours but decades of time. It's a testament to the grit and perseverance of a generation that has continuously adapted to the ever-changing landscape of work.

Over the years, Gen Xers have been considered the steadiest, most independent, and reliable workers—the innovators of work-life balance—and yet they are the last to get promoted. They bear the scarlet "A" of abandonment, often overlooked in organizational planning. But the landscape of the workplace is changing. Companies should favor their adaptable Gen X workers, and employers everywhere should sit up and pay attention.

In this chapter, we'll investigate what is defining Gen X at work today and over the next decade, regardless of their specific job or career. What do employers need to know about this talented cohort, and what do Gen Xers expect as they navigate the super category of Work?

Let's get to Work.

Gen X and the Workforce Reality

There is much written about the impact of Gen Zers as they enter the workforce and the rise of Millennials as they advance in their careers. In 2023, Axios reported Gen Z accounted for 17.1 million workers; Millennials, 49.5 million; Gen X, 42.8 million; and Baby Boomers, 17.3 million.[1] Baby Boomers are leaving the workforce at a rate of 10,000 a day—or 4 million a year—creating a seismic shift. As Gen Z enters the workforce, their total number will exceed that of Boomers beginning 2024.[2] So yes, they will be important in the coming years! However, the primary employment distribution and numbers are dominated by Millennials and Gen X. The key question is: What role will Gen X play in the next decade?

The Gen X+ crowd (i.e., ages 45 to 64) represents 40% of the workforce, up from 28% in 1990. It's estimated that these "older workers" will grow to 57% of the workforce over the next decade.[3]

And this isn't just a US phenomenon. Globally, people are living longer and are generally in much better health. Simultaneously, birth rates in the top economic countries are declining. Together, these trends illustrate the need to keep Gen Xers engaged in the workforce. Consider the chart below for the Group of Seven (G7) countries. The share of aged 55+ workers is expected to increase everywhere but Canada. In 2031, the youngest members of Gen X will only be 51 years old, likely in their prime earning years and critical to the workforce.

The following chart shows the share of workers aged 55 and older in 2011, 2021, and predicted for 2031.

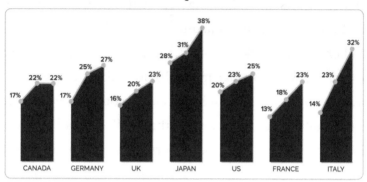

Data pulled from US Bureau of Labor Statistics.

This pronounced shift in workforce ages is good news for many Gen Xers. Anyone whose house sign is X should welcome this "winter is coming" population trend! In theory, a first gray or white hair shouldn't be a death knell to those who want to—or must—work. Human Resources teams and Organizational Design Experts need to socialize this workforce shift and reinforce hiring and promotion practices that keep Gen Xers engaged, or they may be stuck with openings they cannot fill.

How Old Is the Corner Office?

Today, Gen X is not just a core contributor to the overall workforce numbers; it is dominating in overall leadership. In June 2023, *Fortune* reported that Gen X held 267 CEO spots

(53% of the Fortune 500!).[4] Millennials accounted for just 1% (e.g., Meta's Mark Zuckerberg).

But it's not just that top spot. Gen X is populating the full C-suite. The following chart shows the average age of the C-suite executives from the largest 1,000 US companies (by revenue) in 2024 (data analyzed by Korn Ferry).

If these C-suite execs don't officially retire until age 62 or 65, they will be around in some capacity into the 2030s! This is great news for this top percentage of Gen Xers. In fact, it is these Gen Xers who must be change agents for the future talent makeup of their companies. The conundrum is that many industries are fine with having individuals over 50 years old in the C-suite but not in middle management. Age bias, intentional or not, is real, and we are at a crucial tipping point where our views on work and age need to change.

How Old Is Old?

When should you have "made it" in your career? This perception varies, but it's a question many Gen Xers grapple with.

> "It seems like everyone is always on the move, and each job is better than the last! After 10 years at my company, I'm a VP, but then I see a 25-year-old with a VP title, and it makes me feel like I am falling behind. Guess every company has different levels, but what happens when I look for my next job?"
>
> —GEN X ENGINEER, AGE 49

While career progression varies by industry and company, LinkedIn's evolution has put job titles, levels, and promotions front and center. It's all too easy to compare yourself to college friends and professional peers. We're coining a new term: *work dysmorphia.* Like body dysmorphia, where individuals perceive themselves as being physically different from others in an unfavorable way, work dysmorphia leaves individuals unsure if they've truly "made it" professionally.

Let's face it: You can often guess someone's age from their college graduation date or by tallying up their LinkedIn job history. This unconscious age bias affects us all, but surely HR managers and hiring professionals are immune, right?

Wrong. A 2023 study and report by the OECD and Generation (a global employment nonprofit) revealed ingrained ageist attitudes in the business world. Employers often view professionals over 45 as lacking drive and innovation openness. Paradoxically, they also admit this group consistently matches or outperforms younger colleagues. Researchers dub this the "age-performance paradox."[5]

Surprisingly, age 45—which includes some of the youngest Gen Xers today—seems far too young to be considered "past prime." We can't name any friends or colleagues who felt washed up or ready to leave the workforce at 45. Even those who struck it rich in tech kept working.

So, How Does Ageism Impact Gen X Workers?

Popular, dynamic industries tend to attract an up-and-coming talent pool. When Gen Xers were graduating college, they were looking for the newest industries and job opportunities. Remember the dot-com boom, tech explosion, new private equity/venture capital roles in finance, and the rise of digital advertising? Yep, Gen X was straight out of college and immediately began disrupting those industries. But what about now?

There is surprising research on the age distribution in fast-paced industries such as tech and advertising. As we've mentioned, many of the prominent tech founders and CEOs are actually Gen Xers, including Jeff Bezos of Amazon and Sergey Brin of Google, among others. It would be natural to assume that their companies, and the tech industry in general, might embrace a more age-diverse workforce. However, the average age across Google, Amazon, and Meta is a Millennial range of 28 to 33. It is estimated that Gen X accounts for 20% to

25% of the workforce at Google and Meta. The representation is relatively strong for Gen Xers aged 45 to 50, but after 50 years old, their percentage of the workforce drops significantly, falling to around 10%.

The Society for Human Resource Management found that 40% of hiring professionals polled said age affected decisions made during the job application process.[6] For companies offering diversity, equity, and inclusion (DEI) training, only 26% of employers admitted age bias. That's better but not stellar.

Looking at another industry, advertising, the numbers tell a story that's even worse.[7] Over 59% of ad industry employees are between the ages of 25 and 44, with a median age of 38.[8] And this percentage is consistent globally. A 2023 survey of 3,000 UK marketers found that almost three-quarters were between the ages of 26 and 45, and almost half were under 35.[9] In the US, *Forbes* reported that only 5% of ad agency employees were over 50, and most of them were not in creative roles.[10]

These are sobering statistics that may actually run counter to running a successful business. The OECD and Generation report mentioned earlier went as far as to encourage the business world to rethink the current classification of mid-career years as being from ages 45 to 54 and extend the upper end of that range to age 60. This especially makes sense as more seasoned employees can help bridge business and marketplace changes.

- **Productivity:** The OECD reports that companies with a diverse age range have higher productivity rates than similar companies. And older workers' experience can help younger workers perform better, which can further increase productivity. A 2023 working paper from Boston College's Center for Retirement Research also found that older workers are generally as productive as younger workers.

- **Efficiency:** Older workers can bring experience, know-how, reliability, and other qualities that can help companies run more efficiently and save money.

- **Labor Shortages:** Hiring and keeping older workers could help companies prepare for future labor shortages that are expected to occur globally.

How do companies show a return for keeping and recruiting a "mature" Gen X workforce over 45 and 50? Along with ensuring these senior staffers have higher salaries than new hires just entering the workforce, companies need to highlight the gains in productivity and efficiency, as well as avoiding labor force gaps as ROI rationale.

X-perts Weigh In

Gen X—those dedicated workers who have spent decades adapting to an ever-changing workforce—are now facing new challenges in a world of shifting hiring practices accelerated by technological advances like AI. Indeed's Skills-First Hiring initiative is designed to meet these challenges by focusing on what really matters: skills. For a generation that has logged countless hours, endured "Manic Mondays," and been the steadiest contributors to the workplace, this approach offers a level of equity that's long overdue.

As industries shift and age bias persists, Skills-First Hiring ensures that Gen X workers, with their wealth of experience, are valued for what they bring to the table—beyond degrees and outdated job titles. By focusing on skills, not age or traditional credentials, companies can access this adaptable, resilient generation that still has plenty to offer.

Indeed's approach isn't just about filling roles; it's about ensuring diversity and equity at all levels, keeping Gen X engaged, and creating a more inclusive workforce for everyone. In a world where ageism lingers, Skills-First Hiring gives Gen X the recognition they've earned.

—Aidan McLaughlin
Global Director, ESG Marketing
Indeed

Where Are the Corporate Role Models?

Bain & Company's report titled "Better with Age: The Rising Importance of Older Workers" says, "The good news is that, with the right tool kit and mindset, aging workforces can help employers get ahead of their talent gaps and create high-quality jobs that turn older workers' skills into sources of competitive advantage."[11] We identified a few innovative corporate initiatives popping up that should give Gen X hope and inspire other organizations.

> "With dynamic careers lasting longer than ever, our L'Oréal for All Generations initiative acknowledges that we are at a unique moment in history when four generations are working together. In this new environment, where age inclusivity will be vital, we must not only recruit and develop talent at all stages of their careers with well-being benefits to match but also create opportunities for people to exchange their valuable knowledge and experiences with enthusiasm. As someone who has been building a career for nearly 40 years, I personally welcome this evolution."
>
> —DAVID GREENBERG, CEO OF L'ORÉAL USA AND PRESIDENT OF THE COMPANY'S NORTH AMERICA ZONE

L'Oréal, the world leader in beauty—makeup, cosmetics, hair care, and perfumes—has over 85,000 employees. They implemented the L'Oréal for All Generations recruitment and career development program. The rationale for starting the initiative was indeed the workforce-shift data. They recognized that by 2035, 50% of Europe (their headquarters are in France) will be over 45, and 70% of the professions we'll need then don't exist today. Their program taps into intergenerational diversity, health, and well-being; employability/training; and even transition post-L'Oréal employment. Today, 15% of their workforce is over 50 years old. Clearly, L'Oréal views having seasoned Gen X workers as a competitive advantage.

Another example comes from Allianz Group, one of the largest asset management and insurance companies, with over 157,000 employees. They developed Allianz Engage, which focuses on supporting lifelong learning, supporting knowledge transfer between generations, opening a dialogue on what it means to manage and work on age-diverse teams, as well as bringing different experiences and mindsets into the organization.[12] The program is designed to maximize age diversity across all generations and to leverage talent at all career stages. While they do report that Millennials make up the largest percentage of their workforce, they also note Gen Xers represent a significant portion of employee distribution. According to Allianz's *People Fact Book 2022*, employees aged 45 to 54 represent 23% of the workforce, while those aged 50 and above make up 26%.[13]

In both of these examples, we see progressive companies committed to increasing the percentages of older employees. We anticipate that more companies will follow these playbooks, and Gen X talent can find their impact there.

In the meantime, a big shout-out to those current C-suite Gen Xers! They need to be the drivers of change at their companies. No one is in a better position to start the discussion about a generationally distributed workforce. Do it, Gen X!

We Are Stuck in the 20th Century

One of the biggest challenges Gen X faces today is that many employers use outdated 20th-century systems to deal with 21st-century work realities. The Social Security system, while beneficial in many ways, illustrates how our approach to retirement hasn't kept pace with demographic changes. Gen Xers grew up paying into Social Security with each paycheck, expecting monthly payments upon retirement. Currently, the retirement age typically falls between 62 and 67 years old. Legally, Social Security contributors can start to access payments at 62, but full retirement payments don't occur until 67. However, when the US government created Social Security in the 1930s, the average American's life expectancy was only 62 years. While Social Security provided a financial pathway for many lifelong workers, most people in the 1930s didn't live long enough to enjoy much of the program's benefits.

According to the United Nations Population Division's 2022 Revision of World Population Prospects, the life expectancy at birth in the United States is 79.25 years as of 2024.[14] This significant increase in longevity means the legacy retirement mentality no longer matches our viability or long-term financial needs.

The government's adherence to outdated Social Security rules inadvertently encourages early retirement, often before it's financially prudent. These rules influence employers and human resources teams to assume employees are ready to wind down as they approach their late 50s. This mindset can push people out of employment prematurely, potentially jeopardizing their financial security. In short, Gen Xers are concerned about outliving their money.

While significant changes to Social Security are unlikely in the near future, forward-thinking companies must prepare for the coming seismic workforce shift. They need to implement programs that effectively utilize their older demographics, recognizing the value and potential of experienced workers beyond the traditional retirement age.

Work Models and Adaptability

> "While attending the parents' orientation for my college freshman, the dean asked, 'How many jobs will this class have by the time they are 35 years old?' I turned to my husband and said '10,' but the correct answer was 13. I have had 10 in my career thus far, so I guess it makes sense."
>
> —GEN X MOM, AGE 54

The myth that we all work for one company and retire from that company with glorious pensions is long gone. Gen X was really the first generation to experience this "new normal." The Bureau of Labor Statistics reported in 2024 that the average tenure in management and professional occupations is 4.8 years.[15] This further points to the need for companies to take advantage of Gen X and shift their mindsets. In 2025, the youngest Gen Xer will be 45 and might have three more jobs before they retire.

However, these jobs might look and feel different from earlier roles in terms of remote versus onsite work, self-employment, compensation demands, and more. The global pandemic certainly impacted the world of work, and the long-term effects are still playing out.

Let's look at what we know about today's reality for Gen X after the pandemic. The majority were well into their careers during the height of COVID in 2020 through 2022. We mentioned earlier that one reason many Gen Xers fared better financially was because they already owned their homes and were able to comfortably transition to work-from-home demands. Fast-forward to today, and we see that Gen Xers are just as well suited for remote work as members of any younger generation.

Additionally, having grown up in the age of "9 to 5" in the office, Gen Xers are likely not as bothered by back-to-office mandates, which some companies are implementing. It remains to be seen how many employees will be required to work onsite like in days past, but either way, Gen Xers will be fine.

Another work element being tested these days is paid time off (PTO). Here we see a different mindset for Gen Xers. It seems most don't truly unplug. According to LinkedIn's 2024 Workforce Confidence survey, 61% of Gen Xers still read their emails, answer work calls, or otherwise check in with their teams while taking time off. Only 44% of Gen Zers will check in while on PTO.[16] While perhaps not as healthy, Gen Xers appear less protective about their time off and accept that work and life are more intertwined. This behavior may help Gen Xers become more comfortable with developing a side gig while still working full-time or considering a different future work model.

Pioneering Work 2.0: Side Hustles and More

The definitions of work, both jobs and careers, have rapidly evolved in the last decade. It's no longer taboo to get paid for work outside your full-time job. This shift has given rise to side hustles, which fit into the broader gig and creator economies. The gig economy is a labor market focused on short-term contracts, freelance work, and on-demand services. The creator economy, on the other hand, revolves around individuals who create digital content and monetize it directly through platforms such as YouTube, TikTok, Patreon, and Instagram. Both can lead to side hustles, but for Gen Xers, they often leverage career experience or personal passions.

Popular Side Hustles and Potential Revenue

Companies like UpFlip provide valuable insights into potential earnings, start-up costs, and time to profitability for various side hustles.[17] Some popular options include the following:

- **Online Sales:** Monetize creativity on platforms such as Etsy, Shopify, Poshmark, Amazon, and eBay. Average annual revenue: $60K–$120K

- **Freelancing:** Use existing skills in writing, design, teaching, etc., on platforms such as Fiverr, Upwork, and Guru. Average annual revenue: $35K–$150K

- **Online Coaching and Teaching:** Use teaching or mentoring expertise on platforms such as Udemy, Coursera, and LinkedIn Learning. Average annual revenue: $63K+

Gen Xers are particularly well-suited for side hustles. Some come to them with business expertise, while others have an innate ability to identify a need. Consider the journey of Shelly Gates, a 49-year-old Mississippi teacher. After designing her daughter's dorm room and posting pictures on social media, other parents began hiring her for their children's dorm designs. Now she charges $5,000 per room, having turned her talent into a lucrative side business.[18]

The 2022 Zapier "side hustle" report estimated that nearly 38% of Gen Xers have an extra job, with many spending over 10 hours a week on these ventures.[19] Gen Xers know it has never been easier to start a side hustle, thanks to DIY technology. Free open-source tools, software trials, and artificial intelligence make getting started more accessible than ever. If a venture takes off, entrepreneurs can upgrade beyond the free versions. Building a business online also democratizes the playing field, as customers often can't tell if they're dealing with a one-person shop or a large company.

> "Never thought my love of cars would become a side hustle. I built a local repair offering online, and now I have five freelance repair techs working for me. Technology let me set up this side hustle in under 60 days, even while working full time in my sales job."
>
> —GEN X GEARHEAD, AGE 46

Recognizing this potential, some forward-thinking brands are actively targeting older or more mature segments and sensibilities. A few highlighted Gen X-aged entrepreneurs:

- Adobe launched the "Generation X Creator" campaign in 2021. It highlighted Gen X-aged creatives using Adobe's suite of products.

- Squarespace ran the "Build It Beautiful" campaign from 2020 to 2022, featuring testimonials from Gen X-aged business owners who built successful websites on their platform.

- LegalZoom's "Start Your Business" campaign targeted Gen X-aged professionals and small-business owners, emphasizing the ease of managing legal documents online.

Career Transition and Flexibility

So, how do brands attract Gen Xers with side hustles? They should start by understanding what's driving them:

- **Desire for Independence:** Gen Xers value independence and are maybe using side hustles to explore new career paths or passions.

- **Job-Security Concerns:** With AI and shifting job markets, some Gen Xers worry about job security in their primary careers. A side hustle can act as a safety net in case of job loss or career changes.

- **Transitional Employment:** A side hustle can serve as a bridge between traditional full-time jobs or an alternative to retirement.

- **Savings Boost:** Side hustles offer a way to boost retirement savings and reduce debt, especially given that Gen X is closer to retirement age than younger generations.

- **Lingering Economic Caution:** Gen Xers haven't forgotten the instability of the Great Recession and the chaos surrounding the recent pandemic, so they are driven to seek additional financial security before the next economic turn.

- **Sandwich Generation Responsibilities:** Many Gen Xers are caring for both their children and aging parents. Side hustles provide the additional income needed to support these dual responsibilities.

The Rise of Fractional Work

Okay, isn't *fractional* just a fancy word for doing consulting, project work, or part-time work? Yes, but it has taken on a life of its own, and Gen X just might be the true OG.

Here's a short primer on this work phase: In the 2010s, the term *fractional* became more common as the gig economy expanded. Companies like WeWork and Upwork popularized the idea of flexible work arrangements, and professionals increasingly began to seek out fractional roles. Still, the broader workforce primarily used "consulting" or "part-time" to describe these roles.

In the early 2020s, fractional work gained mainstream recognition, and COVID-19 accelerated the demand for flexible, high-skill work arrangements. Not knowing when or how the pandemic would end, employers sought flexible staffing solutions, and many professionals reconsidered traditional full-time employment. Fractional workers became, and continue to be, a great talent source for small and medium-sized businesses.

The trend became official by 2022, with publications such as *Harvard Business Review* and *Forbes* and companies such as LinkedIn using the term regularly. In fact, in McKinsey's 2022 American Opportunity Survey, a full 36% of employed respondents—roughly 58 million Americans—identify as independent workers.[20] The term *fractional* in job titles is growing on Indeed, the world's largest job-search platform. Executive recruiting firms like True Search and Korn Ferry have set up fractional practices to place professionals in these interim roles.

Gen Xers are well-positioned to excel in fractional work, leveraging their significant experience to run projects or serve as interim executives. Many Gen Xers transition to fractional roles after leaving full-time positions, either due to job market challenges or a desire for autonomy. Over 60% of independent workers view fractional work as a long-term career path, appreciating its flexibility and variety compared with traditional roles.[21]

> "Using my previous experience, I sat down and documented how I had built strategic plans across brand, demand gen, digital experience, and marketing operations. As a CMO, I used to hire agencies and freelancers; now it's me. I established an LLC and went fractional."
>
> —GEN X FRACTIONAL CMO, AGE 50

Gen X is poised to define and evolve fractional work. This path requires an entrepreneurial mindset, self-managed benefits, fee negotiation skills, and comfort with job uncertainty. Despite these challenges, it's an attractive option for Gen Xers not ready for retirement or those bridging to their next full-time role.

Employers can benefit from tapping into this skilled workforce. They should actively search for fractional workers on LinkedIn and through organizations such as CHIEF to access expertise they might not otherwise afford. Headhunting firms can increase profitability by establishing fractional placement practices and developing specialized databases.

It's Not You; It's Me

Sometimes we just want change. Many Gen Xers have been working in the same industry for a minimum of 20+ years. And fun fact: They are successful at change. A study performed by the American Institute for Economic Research (AIER) found that 82% of individuals over the age of 47 who attempted a career change after they turned 45 were successful.[22] It might also be surprising to learn that the average age of individuals in nonprofit leadership roles, as well as adjunct professors, franchise owners, and board members, is mid-40s to early/mid-50s! The exact sweet spot for today's Gen Xer.

- The Nonprofit Leadership Alliance suggests that the typical age for executive directors and other senior management roles in nonprofits is around 50 years old.[23]

- The TIAA Institute found that adjunct faculty members often have extensive work experience, with many being in their late 40s or older.[24]

- Guidant Financial reports that 31% of franchise owners fall within the 45 to 54 age range.[25]

- Spencer Stuart reported the average age of new public board members appointed to S&P 500 companies was 57 years old, and BoardSource reported that nonprofit board members are in their mid-40s to early 50s.[26]

"I spent more than 20 years rising to be an SVP at my manufacturing company, and then I invested in a medical concierge franchise. Now I am the CEO and love the total change."

—GEN X MALE, AGE 56

We've said it before and we'll say it again: Gen Xers are lifelong learners, independent, and adaptable. Employers should look to them as an incredible resource, and Gen Xers themselves should be comfortable in taking a risk with work.

Conclusion: The Gen X Work Opportunity

Generation X's approach to work represents a significant shift from that of previous generations, and they push against preconceived trends. This generation is redefining the age paradox of how long we work, where we work, and for whom we work. Gen Xers are also eschewing the traditional retirement route. Many are putting plans in place to keep cash flow coming in for years beyond the fabled retirement age of 62.

For businesses, Gen X is not only a "nice to have" but a *must-have* in order to maintain a workforce and remain competitive. Ignoring Gen X is short-term thinking that can leave companies without leadership, stability, or promising recurring revenue. Companies that ignore this talent pool will quickly find themselves limited as the inevitable workforce shift occurs. The classic mistake is to think those who have served for the longest and who have the biggest salaries are the best individuals to cut during business downturns.

Gen Xers aren't just part of your workforce; they may also be your best customers. Companies selling solutions to small businesses and entrepreneurs will miss out on revenue if they leave Gen Xers off their go-to-market strategies.

The work-life journey is a long one, and it is doubtful Gen X is walking away at 60. With the new options and an evolving employment landscape, Gen Xers will reconstruct their approach to work so that Mondays are less manic. And as we'll see in the next chapter, their work plans will fuel their wealth building and dim the need to "wish it were Sunday."

X FACTOR TAKEAWAYS
Winning with Gen X and Work

- **Prepare for Demographic Shifts:** Recognize the upcoming seismic shift in workforce demographics. With Baby Boomers retiring and fewer younger workers available, keeping Gen Xers engaged in the workforce is not simply beneficial; it's *crucial* for maintaining a stable and experienced workforce.

- **Embrace Age Diversity:** Implement strategies to attract, retain, and motivate employees across all age groups, with a particular focus on leveraging the experience and skills of Gen X workers (aged 45 to 60 in 2025).

- **Redefine Career Trajectories:** Understand that Gen Xers may not follow traditional retirement paths. Develop strategies to accommodate and benefit from their desire for long-term engagement through fractional roles, consulting positions, or part-time/advisory roles.

- **Adapt to Flexible Work Models:** Offer diverse work arrangements, including remote work, mentoring roles, flexible hours, and paths to supporting their transition from side hustles to full-fledged businesses and boards. Companies may find that flexibility outweighs compensation as a top priority.

- **Target Gen X Entrepreneurs:** Companies offering services and products for entrepreneurs should aggressively target Gen X side hustlers. This generation has the experience, financial means, and motivation to turn side gigs into sustainable businesses. Tailor innovative digital marketing strategies and product offerings to support their entrepreneurial journey.

CHAPTER 7

Wealth

"Sweet Dreams (Are Made of This)"
—Eurythmics (1983)

"In this country," the character Tony Montana famously says in *Scarface*, "you gotta make the money first. Then when you get the money, you get the power." Not that we'd ever want to cross Tony Montana, but he's only covering part of the story.

Wealth encompasses more than just money. One might have a lot of cash on hand but be a paycheck away from bankruptcy in terms of net worth, or wealth. Wealth is the long game of personal financial security that ties today's reality to tomorrow's dreams.

US News & World Report offers the following equation for determining wealth: "To calculate your net worth, add up the market value of all your assets. These often include cash and the current value of your investment accounts, equity in real estate, vehicles, personal property, and cash value life insurance policies. Then, tally all of your debts, like what you might owe on credit cards and loans, and subtract that number from your assets."[1] In layman's terms, wealth (or net worth) is what remains after subtracting all debts from all assets.

In this chapter, we'll see why Gen X is poised to build wealth and how brands can better target them to see X Factor growth. A few chapters ago, we looked at the economic cycles and how they played a role in the amount of money Gen Xers had to invest, buy, and save. In the last chapter, we dove into that pesky little reality that's true for most of us when it comes to wealth: You've gotta work to get it. Tony Montana was on the right track. For any Gen Xer looking to grow their net worth by acquiring assets, their money is the key to success.

The song "Sweet Dreams" is a great metaphor for what overall wealth can deliver. Do Gen Xers have enough wealth to maintain their lifestyles today and still make their dreams come true? Sending kids to college, buying a house or boat, quitting their job, or traveling the world and the seven seas? Everybody's looking for something.

Is Gen X Wealthy?

According to Edelman Financial Engines' "Everyday Wealth in America 2023 Report," four out of five Americans say "being financially secure enough to not worry about money" is their main driver for building wealth.

However, very few Americans consider themselves wealthy. This report reveals that only 14% of them believe they are wealthy. Even among the affluent—those with household assets ranging from $500,000 to $3 million and who are working with a financial professional—fewer than one in five describe themselves as "wealthy."[2]

> **"It's so hard to know what is wealthy. I thought I would know the answer as I got older. Now, I am actually embarrassed to ask questions. Everything I read or hear makes me more confused. I think I am well off, but who knows."**
>
> —GEN X OPS MANAGER, AGE 51

For our purposes, we want to determine how Gen X feels about their wealth and what they are doing about it. The following chart illustrates the inverse relationship between individuals in the pre-50 age groups and those over 50. It illustrates the difference between the level of assets it takes to feel wealthy compared with how much it takes to be worry-free. The "delta" depends greatly on age and gives us some insight into the psyches of Gen Xers. The money difference between being worried and being worry-free is highest for those in their 30s and 40s. Being worry-free takes more money (peaking at nearly $1 million). For those in their 60s and beyond, however, the numbers flip-flop: it takes more to feel wealthy than it does to be worry-free.

Level of Assets Needed to Feel Wealthy vs Never Worry About Money

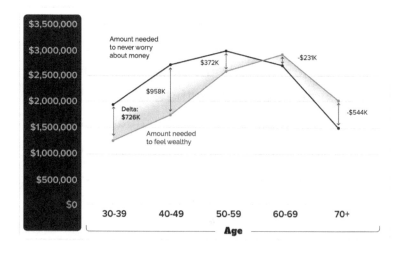

The perception of wealth often differs between generations, particularly in how they view immediate income versus long-term assets. Younger Americans tend to prioritize tangible cash and monthly salaries. However, as Scott Galloway explains in his book *The Algebra of Wealth,* true wealth occurs when "passive income exceeds your burn." This concept challenges the notion that a high salary alone equates to financial security. For instance, someone earning $1 million annually but spending $1.2 million is actually worse off financially than an individual who has a smaller salary but has fewer expenses and invests a portion into long-term assets like real estate, stocks, or retirement accounts. What did our parents say . . . don't spend beyond your means?

Galloway further defines wealth as "the absence of economic stress in life." This perspective is particularly relevant for Gen Xers as they approach the traditional retirement age. The key question becomes: As Gen Xers transition away from regular salaries, will the wealth they've accumulated provide them with financial peace of mind? This stress-free financial state is the ultimate goal, emphasizing the importance of building sustainable wealth rather than simply chasing high incomes.

So, what is the amount needed to feel "wealthy"? According to the Charles Schwab Modern Wealth Survey 2023, overall, Americans believe it takes $2.2 million in net worth to be considered wealthy. The survey determined that $10.2 million is considered the threshold for being "very wealthy."[3]

Whether Gen Xers believe they are wealthy or not, the fact is, they control close to 30% of the nation's net wealth, and many of them are still in their peak earning years. The chart below shows the trillions of dollars associated with each generation today.

Generation	Assets	Liabilities	Wealth	Share of Wealth
Silent Generation	$18.6	$0.8	$17.8	13%
Baby Boomers	$78.1	$5.1	$73.0	53%
Generation X	$46.0	$7.0	$39.0	28%
Millenials	$13.3	$5.5	$7.8	6%
Total	$156.0	$18.4	$137.6	100%

The amount of wealth is expected to expand, which makes Gen X a key target for the wealth management industry, especially as Baby Boomers and the Silent Generation pass away. In fact, it is estimated that Gen Xers will be the greatest immediate recipients of what is called the Great Wealth Transfer.

The Great Wealth Transfer and Gen X

There is much written about the Great Wealth Transfer: Is it coming, who gets it, when will it happen, and how much is it? Economists have estimated the transfer will exceed $84 trillion over the next 20 years. According to Cerulli Associates, $72 trillion is expected to transfer to heirs, while $12 trillion is expected to go to philanthropy.[4] Amounts and timing vary, but let's look at what portion of this wealth is likely to land in the pockets and portfolios of Gen Xers.

According to the same Cerulli data, the following is the breakdown of the Great Wealth Transfer with the estimated generational wealth to be inherited through 2045. Gen X is set to receive the most.

- Baby Boomers (born 1946–1964) will inherit $4 trillion.

- Gen X (1965–1980) will inherit $30 trillion.

- Millennials (1981–1996) will inherit $27 trillion.

- Gen Z (1997–2012) or younger will inherit $11 trillion.

"This [wealth transfer] is not about Boomers and Millennials. Assuming most people die by 80 or 85, and that the adult children of the Silent Generation are today around age 50, most of the inherited assets will go to Gen Xers. People who inherit $500,000 are often experienced with financial services, with 35% having taxable brokerages and generally having higher levels of equity in real estate than average."

—LAURA VARAS, CEO AND FOUNDER OF HEARTS & WALLETS

So how does the $30 trillion of Gen X inheritance break down? According to Wealth-X, the average age of individuals in North America set to inherit fortunes from parents worth $5 million or more is 46.1 years old.[5] The findings cast a spotlight on the large wealth potential for Gen X, which has been largely overlooked in the discussion of young inheritors. It is currently estimated that Millennial and Gen Z grandchildren will likely receive smaller individual amounts, while Gen X children are expected to inherit larger shares.

Given the impending largest generational wealth transfer in history, Gen X stands to become a formidable force in the wealth management industry. Companies and financial brands must prioritize this demographic to capitalize on this unprecedented opportunity. In wealth management, assets under management (AUM) is a crucial success metric. AUM is the total market value of investments (can be bank deposits, mutual funds, cash, stocks, bonds, and even treasure notes) that a company or individual manages. This massive transfer of wealth positions Gen Xers to significantly increase their asset acquisition. Focusing on Gen X is not simply strategic; it is essential for any firm aiming to expand its business and secure its future in the industry.

Buying Power versus Spending Power

When discussing wealth, economists and financial reporters often talk about buying power for investing versus spending power in cash for general purchases. Buying power in investing is the amount of money an investor has on hand to buy securities, stocks, cryptocurrency, options, or any other financial instrument.

And Gen X has significant sums on hand. With over $357 billion of buying power today, this generation is and should be a prime target for financial advisors. As discussed in Chapter 3, Gen X has lived through the various market cycles of the dot-com bubble (1995–2000), the Great Recession (2007–2009), and the COVID-19 pandemic (2020–2023), and they have seen their investment portfolios bounce back.

For the bounce back perspective, consider that as of September 2023, the S&P 500 was up nearly 394% since 2009. Following the 2008 crisis, lower interest rates, bond buying by the central bank, quantitative easing (QE), and the rise of the FAANG stocks added market value to global stock markets.[6]

> **"My parents stressed saving because that's what they did, and it was enough. Thank goodness my first boss insisted I max out my 401(k) and invest in funds and ETFs. The magic of reinvesting dividends and letting it grow is going to save me later."**
>
> —GEN X CUSTOMER SERVICE MANAGER, AGE 47

On the surface, Gen Xers appear to be more comfortable with traditional asset classes since their portfolios and 401(k)s rebounded. Assets allocated to exchange-traded funds (ETFs) are more than $7.6 trillion in 2023, up from $0.8 trillion in 2008, according to GWI. Traditional stocks and bonds are considered vital to a strong investment strategy by 68% of Gen X+. In fact, 55% of their investment portfolios is with stocks and bonds. This feels intuitive given the earlier financial cycles they experienced, with stocks delivering such a strong net growth. This is, however, a stark contrast to Gen Z and Millennials, with 75% agreeing or strongly agreeing that "it's not possible to achieve above-average returns solely with traditional stocks and bonds."[7]

However, don't be fooled into thinking that Gen Xers are simply cautious, risk-averse wealth builders. They are also key drivers in the growth of alternative investments. Alternative investments are supplemental strategies to traditional long-only positions in stocks, bonds, and cash. Alternatives include investments in five main categories: hedge funds, private capital, natural resources, real estate, and infrastructure. A Bank of America report highlighted that 31% of Gen X identified real estate as the greatest opportunity for growth, 21% favored international equities, and 15% saw private equity as the best option.[8]

This diverse range of financial vehicles provides ample opportunities to target the $357 billion buying power of this generation. Given this buying power, it is surprising we don't see more Gen X-specific marketing efforts beyond thought leadership content. It's definitely an untapped opportunity for wealth management firms and financial services overall.

The Gen X Emotional Wealth Persona

Building wealth is not all about the numbers. There is also an emotional component. If we were to pick up a sociological magnifying glass, we might find that Gen X harbors a particularly interesting combination of confidence and caution.

According to the US Bureau of Labor Statistics, the median income of American workers is highest between ages 45 and 54. These peak earning years are a critical time to take control of finances and hone money management strategies. This is the current sweet spot for Gen X in 2025, but it might be surprising to learn they are not as confident as one would think. The data from the US Bureau of Labor Statistics illustrates Gen X sentiment overall.

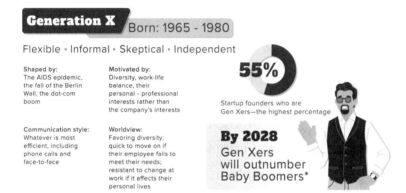

Generation X Born: 1965 - 1980

Flexible • Informal • Skeptical • Independent

Shaped by:
The AIDS epidemic, the fall of the Berlin Wall, the dot-com boom

Motivated by:
Diversity, work-life balance, their personal - professional interests rather than the company's interests

Communication style:
Whatever is most efficient, including phone calls and face-to-face

Worldview:
Favoring diversity; quick to move on if their employee fails to meet their needs; resistant to change at work if it affects their personal lives

55%
Startup founders who are Gen Xers—the highest percentage

By 2028
Gen Xers will outnumber Baby Boomers*

Chart re-designed based on graphic and data from US Bureau of Labor Statistics.

But how does this persona relate to their buying power and actions?

Multiple recent studies have been conducted by the wealth-tech corporation of Envestnet, where they studied what they call Intelligent Financial Life™.[9] They assert that the ability to live an "Intelligent Financial Life" starts with understanding what people need in their daily financial lives, as well as their future ones. The studies were designed to uncover what investors of all ages really want, need, expect, and hope will be provided to guide them on their journey toward financial well-being. Looking at the Gen X data provides us with a blueprint for understanding and reaching this segment.

> "By connecting people's daily financial lives to their long-term goals, you can help people navigate the needs they have today to where they want to go tomorrow—providing the tools and strategies that give people more visibility, generating more awareness, helping people grow financial confidence as they progress and check off the milestones on their way to achieve their goals."
>
> —BILL CRAGER, ENVESTNET CO-FOUNDER AND FORMER CEO

Given the economic and financial cycles Gen Xers have experienced, their emotional view of money and wealth is understandably mixed. According to the same Envestnet study just mentioned, despite Gen Xers having significant wealth, when asked about their finances, 39% were stressed, 28% were anxious, and only 28% were hopeful. All these descriptors speak to a group of individuals who are craving guidance. In fact, 73% reported being skeptical about retirement and welcomed financial planning.

Am I Keeping Up with the Joneses?

The age-old question "How am I doing compared to others?" inevitably surfaces when discussing wealth. It is often advised to avoid discussing "money, politics, and religion" at social gatherings. This social taboo might explain why many Gen Xers are uncertain about their financial standing. Wealth often remains a topic reserved for private conversations with close family members or financial advisors, or solitary late-night internet searches.

Remember the term *work dysmorphia* from Chapter 6? Interestingly, about 25% of Gen Xers might be experiencing what's known as *money dysmorphia*. While not an official diagnosis, this concept describes an irrational insecurity about one's finances. Financial planning experts warn that this mindset can lead to poor money decisions, including overspending and making risky investments.[10]

This financial insecurity, whether justified or not, can be exacerbated by social media and broader cultural trends. Edelman's research reveals that 74% of Americans believe people present themselves on social media platforms as being wealthier than they actually are.[11] While money dysmorphia is more commonly associated with Gen Z, it significantly impacts how Gen X perceives and manages their wealth.

Given these challenges, it's clear that Gen Xers could benefit from more information and advice about their financial health. The more accurate and personalized guidance they receive, the better equipped they'll be to assess their true financial position and make informed decisions.

Digital Information and Interaction

The delivery of financial advice is crucial to building and investing wealth. It is important to consider where, how, and by whom this advice is provided. Given that Gen Xers control around $46.7 trillion of assets, you can imagine that all segments of the financial services, banking, and wealth management industry will want to focus on them.[12]

As we explored in Chapter 2, the misconception that Gen X is not digitally savvy persists, particularly in the financial services industry's marketing efforts. This misbelief is starkly contrasted by the rapid growth of the financial technology (fintech) sector. According to *Fortune Business Insights*, fintech is projected to experience a compound annual growth rate (CAGR) of 16.5%, with its global market value expanding from $340.10 billion in 2024 to $1,152.06 billion by 2032.[13] Despite this boom, much of the media attention and targeted research has focused on Gen Z and Millennials. While this approach might build brand awareness for future revenue, the financial industry risks overlooking a significant source of current buying power by not creating information-first digital experiences tailored to Gen X.

The behavioral data tells a different story about Gen X's digital engagement. Alkami Technology's 2024 Generational Trends in Digital Banking Study reveals that 86% of Gen Xers desire a digital banking experience, positioning them squarely between Millennials and Gen Zers in this preference.[14] This statistic may not be surprising given the widespread adoption of digital banking across age groups. Most people, regardless of their generation, now manage their day-to-day transactions digitally. We set up automatic deposits to our bank accounts, check balances, and transfer money swiftly via our smartphones. It's worth noting that even many Baby Boomers have embraced digital banking, further emphasizing the cross-generational appeal of these services.

When Alkami performed their study, they asked the following: *When thinking about your ideal provider, how important is user experience and functionality of the banking website and/or mobile banking app?* The following chart (designed based on the data from Alkami and The Center for Generational Kinetics, LLC) shows how different generations ranked the importance of their digital banking experience. (Percentages who noted "very important" or "important" are reflected. N = 1,500 digital banking consumers.)

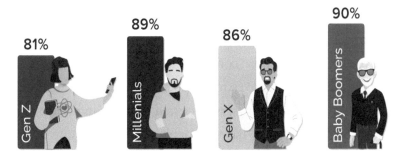

But Gen Xers also dominate in digital payment tech. The same Alkami study referenced that a total of 82% use PayPal for direct payments, and 65% would likely use it for "buy now, pay later" (BNPL) purchases. Given this generation's growing usage of payment technologies, financial institutions need to invest in robust app and digital strategies to keep this group engaged and satisfied.[15]

We are encouraged to see that some financial brands are creatively marketing to the Gen X persona. JPMorgan Chase began running a generational ad called "Meet the Jennifers" to promote its mobile banking app. In the TV spot, Chase calls out the fact that while Gen X Jen is saving for a summer trip to Portugal, Gen Y/Millennial Jen is just saving for her birthday, and Gen Z Jen is in the early stages of saving and building credit for the future.[16] This is smart marketing that speaks directly to each generation, and in our case, directly to the Gen X wealth persona. Snap!

However, this digital demand is not just for quick banking or short-term purchases; it extends to investing too. The mainstream introduction of robo-investing brought investing to everyone, including Gen X, and has helped propel digital financial demands. Robo-advisors—also known as automated investing services—use computer algorithms and software to build and manage investment portfolios. While traditional portfolio management services often require high balances, robo-advisors typically have low or no minimum requirements. Within a matter of minutes online, anyone can get started. Easy, quick, and thorough equals winning online.

In mid-2021, the crypto industry embraced this immediate online behavior and used sophisticated mobile marketing to attract investors. Before we go further, let's align on a cryptocurrency definition. For the layperson, cryptocurrency is a type of digital or virtual currency that uses cryptography for security. Unlike traditional currencies issued by governments (such as the US dollar or the Euro), cryptocurrencies operate on decentralized networks based on blockchain technology—a distributed ledger that records all transactions across a network of computers.

In 2021, crypto was exploding in the mainstream as a new global currency with potentially high returns. Many investors wanted a way into this new financial instrument, so they bought cryptocurrency stocks via easy mobile interfaces. Crypto marketers were creative.

> **"Hey, I thought if Tom Brady and Matt Damon are investing in crypto, then it must be a good place for me too!"**
>
> —GEN X INVESTOR, AGE 51

Remember how we discussed the dot-com Super Bowl XXXIV that took place in 2000? Well, fans called 2022's Super Bowl LVI the "Crypto Bowl"—with ads from FTX, Coinbase, and Crypto.com being the main media buyers. We won't dive into the fact that after both Super Bowls, both dot-coms and cryptocurrencies had some volatility; rather instead, we are highlighting the craving for digital and technology with general finances and investing.

Crypto marketing used gamification go-to-market approaches. The digital interfaces were easy to use, and they motivated people to keep looking at their balances. Investors could track their crypto portfolio or account instantaneously and were excited to see results. Consider that in 2022, 31% of Gen X crypto investors checked their crypto account daily or multiple times a day rather than looking at their bonds/stocks portfolio results quarterly![17]

This points to a massive Gen X digital demand overall and dispels the myth that this generation isn't digital. In fact, 78% of "affluent American Gen Xers" (defined as having a household net worth or income over $100,000) want a *personalized digital financial experience.*[18]

Here's the TL;DR version (a term bequeathed to us by Millennials and their penchant for abbreviation): Gen Xers want to receive targeted, relevant, personalized information via digital. And they want it at every step of wealth building. This could mean a website that responsively adapts to each individual and just shows pertinent information. It could mean the steady drumbeat of pro tips or the next best action for the investor sent via text or email. It could also be the use of AI to generate dedicated information and content.

The list goes on and on. Digital delivery to Gen X is nonnegotiable, but it must still feel personalized and "human."

X-perts Weigh In

Gen X isn't following anyone's script when it comes to wealth, and why should we?

We've been navigating life on our own terms since day one, bucking societal norms and rewriting what success looks like. Wealth for us? It's not just about numbers on a balance sheet. It's about freedom—the freedom to design our lives, support our families in whatever form they take, and invest in futures that align with who we are, not what society expects.

We've seen markets rise and fall, yet here we stand—tech-savvy, skeptical, and resourceful as ever. While everyone else is focused on flashy trends, we're making wealth work for us, blending traditional investments with alternative strategies and digital tools.

For Gen X, the real value of wealth isn't in the accumulation but in how we use it to stay independent, thrive, and keep pushing forward.

Because if there's one thing Gen X knows, it's that we don't fit into anyone's mold. We're still building, still innovating, and we're not done. Wealth management? It's just another arena where we make our own rules.

—Dani Fava
Chief Strategy Officer
Carson Group

Financial Advisors and the Human Connection

We just used a lot of ink outlining why *digital* matters to Gen Xers and their finances. But the human element in wealth management cannot be underestimated either. Enter the financial advisor, the certified financial planner (CFP), the broker, and the whole team.

A substantial 62% of Americans said that having a financial advisor makes them feel significantly more secure in their current financial situation.[19] While the Gen Z kids of Gen Xers might be swayed by the finfluencers (individuals who, by virtue of their popular or cultural status, have the ability to influence the financial decision-making processes of others through promotions or recommendations on social media), their parents often feel more secure with a dedicated professional advisor. Over half of Gen Xers—56%—say they would be more willing to have financial discussions if someone else were to initiate them; 63% of Gen Xers report that they learn by talking to others.[20]

Given Gen Xers' skepticism and caution, the role of the financial advisor—and the human interaction—is critical. This is probably good news for the more than 300K advisors in the United States! In addition to wanting to be updated on the best growth investments, some Gen Xers are at the life stage in which college tuition, long-term care, elder relatives, and their own retirement take on significant importance. Talking to an advisor can be invaluable.

Remember that Great Wealth Transfer we talked about? Gen Xers who receive these dollars will likely need a financial advisor to help them. This could be a huge AUM and revenue win for advisory firms. Consider that over the next 10 years, 1.2 million individuals with $5 million or more will pass down a total of $31 trillion in wealth.[21] Many of those passing along this wealth have it sitting with an advisor. However, there is no guarantee that the Gen X recipient will keep their assets with said advisor, especially if they have no relationship with them. A staggering 70% of women who divorce or whose spouses die move on to other financial advisors.[22] While this doesn't necessarily mean the Great Wealth Transfer will see this much movement, it is a cautionary data point.

History tells us that "what to do with the inherited wealth" isn't a top family conversation. The Edelman Financial Engines' 2023 report mentioned earlier stated that 30% of those receiving inheritances said their parents' gift caused family conflict. They reported that their parents did a poor job of communicating their intentions, and more often than not, this resulted in many headaches, if not all-out brawls.

Getting an infusion of money, at any level, can change the wealth dynamic. Depending on the amount, financial structures such as trusts and estate plans can ensure the protection and growth of the assets. Additionally, there can be tax implications and more. A good CFP can help the Gen Xer navigate these issues and access a team of experts from attorneys to tax accountants. The real opportunity with the Great Wealth

Transfer is for advisors to create a detailed playbook for the Gen X client on what to do on day one and prepare a road map for years to come. This is just another example of why the human element in wealth is crucial.

The Best of Both Worlds

Gen Xers' need for traditional human advisors, coupled with robust digital experiences, may on the surface seem contradictory. But we can no longer disregard their desire to have both online and offline components of wealth building. For Gen Xers, it is not an *either/or;* it's an *and.* Their need for Human-Digital experiences arises again.

The financial services brands that fully embrace this mentality will win. Don't leave the best digital experience and tech innovation to the latest fintech startup, and don't dismiss the value of face-to-face or one-on-one human interactions as only something "old people" want.

> "Look, I can basically manage my life on my phone or computer day to day, but I still want to talk to a person when it counts and certainly when it comes to my wealth plan. Understanding long-term care, alternatives, and IRAs is too important for a Google click spree."
>
> —GEN X FEMALE SALES VP, AGE 50

Conclusion: Gen X Wealth Opportunities

As Gen Xers maximize their peak earning years and near the traditional retirement age, it's clear that their approach to wealth and life transitions differs significantly from that of previous generations. Few from this generation will be receiving the employer pensions that their parents may have had as a nest egg. Gen Xers also differ from those of the younger generations who are pursuing Financial Independence, Retire Early (FIRE) goals or taking financial advice from TikTok finfluencers.

The financial services and wealth management industries have a unique opportunity to cater to Gen Xers' evolving needs. To succeed, these industries must go beyond the basics of wealth transfer administration, risk assessments, and stock portfolio recommendations. The most successful advisors and brands will be those who can match Gen X's flexibility as they are working to be free from financial stress. This includes creating financial strategies for handling life's curveballs: job changes, sandwich generation expenses, and realities that impede net financial worth growth.

This will be especially important for those who haven't accumulated the fabled $1.9 million or whatever their magic "I've made it" number may be.

Looking ahead, the next decade could see Gen X jettison the "forgotten generation" moniker to become the "impact generation." Smart companies can help Gen X right now to make that transition. Wealth, not just money, is the enabler of "Sweet Dreams" for Gen X. Let's be honest: *everybody is looking for something!* Who are we to disagree?

X FACTOR TAKEAWAYS

Growing Wealth with Gen X

- **Inform first and often. This is a prepared group.** Wealth building is complex, and Gen Xers have heard a lot of strategies. They are looking for informative content to guide them at every step. You can reach them in multiple ways, from long-form content to quick text messages. Use a variety of communication channels, but make sure they add value and are actionable.

- **Don't assume they aren't adaptable.** Gen Xers have seen the value of new business models and embraced investment vehicles. Since 45% of their portfolios are outside of stocks and bonds, be sure to talk to them about new opportunities, and be cautious about overusing the term *retirement planning*.

- **Investing and wealth building don't stop at 50 or even 60.** Gen Xers are in their highest earning years and motivated to build. They might just want to invest in growth, in addition to safe value investments, because they plan to live into their 80s and beyond! Ignore them, and they'll invest their big dollars elsewhere.

- **Deliver a Human-Digital experience.** Create a robust experience that uses the best digital features but allows for human interaction. Brands that make Gen Xers feel like they have personalized their wealth journey will win.

CHAPTER 8

Wellness

"Losing My Religion"

—R.E.M. (1991)

As Generation X navigates their 40s and 50s, they're not losing their religion; they're finding a new one: wellness. This cohort is redefining what it means to age gracefully, armed with information, technology, and a determination to stay healthy and vital well into their later years.

Gen Xers' approach to wellness is unique, shaped by their experiences growing up during the rise of the fitness culture in the 1980s and their current position sandwiched between aging parents and growing children. They're tech-savvy enough to embrace new health technologies but old-school enough to value tried-and-true methods of staying healthy.

This chapter will explore the key wellness trends resonating with Gen Xers, from physical fitness and nutrition to mental health and preventative medicine. As this generation enters a new phase of life, they're not simply maintaining their health; they're optimizing it, often with the disposable income to invest in products and services that promise to keep them feeling young and energetic.

For businesses, understanding Gen X's wellness priorities opens up a world of opportunities. This generation is willing to spend on their health and well-being, making them a prime target for innovative wellness products, services, and experiences. Knowing that their "church" may be the Sunday morning bike trek, their favorite hiking trail, a 5K run, or the pickleball court is an insight into a valuable audience.

Physical Fitness

Gen Xers' relationship with fitness has evolved significantly since their teenage years of Jane Fonda workout tapes and Richard Simmons' *Sweatin' to the Oldies*. Now in their 40s and 50s, this generation is redefining what it means to be fit and active in midlife.

Gen Xers make up about 33% of health club members, showing a strong commitment to structured fitness routines.[1] Members of this generation are looking for effective, time-efficient workouts that fit into their busy lives while addressing the unique challenges of maintaining fitness after 40. They really look at fitness as a team sport, with a strong preference over other generations for the group fitness activities often found in gyms and community centers.

Popular fitness trends among Gen X include the following:

1. High-Intensity Interval Training (HIIT): Gen Xers appreciate the efficiency of HIIT workouts, which provide maximum results in minimal time. A survey found that HIIT was among the top three fitness trends for adults aged 40 to 60.[2]

2. Strength Training: Recognizing the importance of maintaining muscle mass as they age, many Gen Xers are incorporating strength training into their routines. Today, only 30% of adults aged 45 to 64 meet the recommended guidelines for muscle-strengthening activities, indicating room for growth in this area.[3]

3. Yoga and Low-Impact Exercise: As Gen Xers become more conscious of joint health and injury prevention, many are turning to yoga and other low-impact exercises. Yoga also helps with balance, flexibility, and core strength to complement their other fitness activities. A 2022 Yoga Alliance study found that 36% of yoga practitioners in the US are between 40 and 54 years old.[4]

"I used to just run for fitness. But after hitting 45, I realized that I also needed core strength to offset all my office chair time and the yoga that helps my flexibility. If I want to run until I'm 80, I need to change up my routine now."

—GEN X RUNNER, AGE 50

Take It Outside

Gen X is also rediscovering the joy of outdoor fitness, with activities like hiking, cycling, and kayaking gaining popularity. Even walking alone or in groups is having its moment. This trend was definitely supercharged during the pandemic, when gyms were closed and the CDC recommended outdoor activities as a safer way to keep active. The Outdoor Industry Association reports that participation in outdoor activities among those aged 45 to 54 increased by 12% in 2022.

Paddleboarding is an outdoor sport that offers a unique combination of physical exercise and relaxation, which appeals to many Gen Xers. It's a full-body workout that improves balance, strength, and endurance, but it's also a serene way to connect with nature, which is particularly appealing for those who grew up in an era before the digital age took over. The low-impact nature of the sport makes it accessible for those who may be looking for a gentler form of exercise without sacrificing the benefits of a robust physical activity.

Pickleball (Of Course!)

And we really can't talk about fitness without commenting on pickleball—the fastest-growing sport in America. The funny thing about pickleball is that it started as an "old folks" sport. It was often referred to as the "new-age shuffleboard." But over the past few years, it caught on, and participants became progressively younger.

Gen Xers, known for their adaptability and desire to maintain an active lifestyle, have found pickleball to be the perfect balance of physical activity and social engagement. The sport's popularity has surged in recent years, particularly among those in their 40s and 50s who appreciate its low-impact nature and the camaraderie it fosters. It ties back to that "fitness is a team sport" mentality.

Statistics underscore the sport's appeal to Gen Xers. Players aged 40 to 54 make up the most active age group in the sport.[5] This is reflective of a broader trend in which Gen X is increasingly prioritizing wellness activities that are both enjoyable and sustainable. With around 50 million adults in the United States having played pickleball at least once in the past 12 months, the sport is more than just a pastime: it's becoming a key component of the Gen X wellness culture.

> **"I don't care if my kids mock my pickleball obsession. It was easy for me to learn. It keeps me active and competitive, and best of all, I'm connected to a really fun group of people who love to play as much as I do."**
>
> —GEN X MOM, AGE 52

Wearable technology and fitness tracking devices have also become integral to Gen X's fitness journey. And yes, most of them now have pickleball settings! According to a report by Pew Research Center, 31% of Americans aged 45 to 54 use a fitness tracker or smartwatch to monitor their health and activity levels.[6] These devices appeal to Gen Xers' data-driven nature, allowing them to set goals, track progress, and compete with friends.

The running joke among Gen X fitness enthusiasts is that if you didn't track it, it didn't happen. Walkers, runners, spin class participants, and others often experience a moment of despair when they realize they left their tracker at home. A healthy obsession? Maybe. And a reminder that wearable tech and apps that provide personalized fitness plans and track age-specific health metrics are good business opportunities.

Workout apps have been another welcome technology for fitness-seeking Gen Xers. With options that range from wall Pilates to Peloton's full set of workouts, these apps offer convenience to the Gen Xer with a busy schedule. Heavily advertised on Instagram and Facebook, the apps employ videos, before-and-after images, and a high volume of ads to encourage individuals to try them out. As most of these apps have a freemium offer that moves to an automatic subscription, their owners probably hope the charge gets lost, forgotten, and renewed.

As Gen Xers continue to prioritize fitness, they're looking for solutions that are effective, time-efficient, and tailored to their changing bodies. Businesses that can meet these needs while tapping into Gen Xers' efforts to stay healthy and youthful are on the right track. When messaging to Gen Xers, the focus should be on "staying fit" rather than framing it as something useful for "someone of your age." Listen up: Talking to a 45-year-old athlete about "being careful with his joints" is a swing and a miss. Framing fitness as a way to achieve health and vitality goals is the way to get Gen Xers on board.

Embracing Wellness in the Gen X Era

As a fitness expert who's witnessed the evolution of health trends, I've observed how Generation X has uniquely positioned itself in the wellness landscape. This generation bridges the gap between traditional fitness methods and modern holistic approaches.

For Gen Xers, wellness isn't just about looking good; it's about feeling good and staying vibrant as they navigate midlife. They're focusing on sustainable practices that nourish both body and mind. They want reliable ways to manage stress, get a good night's sleep, and keep their bodies working well and looking good.

In my studios, we work with Gen X to prioritize functional fitness, emphasizing exercises that build strength and flexibility for near-term results and long-term health. I am also an advocate of Gen X's willingness to balance careers and families with mindfulness and meditation and self-care. Also, as a generation, they are coming around to understanding the power of food as medicine, focusing on anti-inflammatory diets and gut health as part of their nutrition-as-prevention approach.

Like everyone, the Gen Xers in my studios wear fitness apps to monitor progress and stay motivated. But they come from the tradition of group classes and team sports—so they embrace the importance of community in their wellness journey, engaging in group fitness classes and communities that keep us accountable and connected.

Remember, wellness isn't a destination; it's a journey. Gen Xers have the wisdom to know that small, consistent changes lead to significant results. I see them embracing their unique paths to wellness, and they are not afraid to mix traditional methods with cutting-edge approaches. Their best years are still ahead!

—Andrea Metcalf
Founder of FLX Move
Author of *Naked Fitness*
Fitness Influencer and Public Speaker

Nutrition

As Gen Xers navigate midlife, their approach to nutrition is evolving. This generation is increasingly aware of the link between diet and overall health, seeking nutritional solutions that address their changing needs. A 2023 report reveals that 72% of Gen X consumers are actively trying to eat healthier, focusing on managing weight, boosting energy, and preventing chronic diseases.[7] Gone are the days of fad diets and quick fixes; instead, this generation is seeking sustainable, science-backed approaches to eating that support overall health and longevity.

This heightened interest in nutrition presents significant opportunities for food manufacturers, supplement companies, and nutrition-focused services.

Gen X's nutritional interests are diverse and sophisticated. They're increasingly interested in personalized nutrition. As they become more aware of how individual factors, including genetics, lifestyle, and environment, can influence nutritional needs, many are seeking tailored dietary advice. A

Nutrigenomix study found that 64% of adults aged 40 to 60 would be interested in genetic testing to optimize their diet.[8] This has spurred a rise in DNA-based diet plans and customized supplement regimens.

The rise of DNA-based diets and nutrigenomics—the study of how genes interact with nutrition—is particularly appealing to this data-driven generation. Companies offering genetic testing for personalized nutrition recommendations have seen significant growth, with the global nutrigenomics market expected to reach $17.1 billion by 2026.[9]

"Functional" foods are also gaining traction, with Gen Xers seeking ingredients that offer specific health benefits beyond basic nutrition. Examples of functional foods include probiotic yogurt, fortified cereals (enriched with vitamins and minerals), omega-3 enriched eggs, and foods containing added fiber, such as certain breads and snack bars. These foods are designed to offer specific health benefits, such as improving heart health, enhancing digestion, or supporting cognitive function, in addition to their basic nutritional value. The global functional foods market is expected to reach $275.7 billion by the end of 2025, with Gen X as a key consumer segment.

While not necessarily embracing full vegetarianism or veganism, many Gen Xers are incorporating more plant-based options into their diets. A survey by the Plant Based Foods Association found that 39% of Gen X consumers regularly purchase plant-based alternatives, indicating a growing openness to diverse protein sources and plant-centric eating.

> "Sometimes I just crave an old-fashioned beef burger. But the plant-based patties are getting so much better, so I rotate them into our meals. I think they are healthier for me and better for the planet."
>
> —GEN X MOM, AGE 46

Trust Your Gut

One of the most significant nutritional trends among Gen X is the growing awareness of gut health. The gut microbiome—the trillions of bacteria that live in our digestive tract—has emerged as a crucial factor in overall health, influencing everything from digestion to immune function and even mental health.

A survey by the International Food Information Council found that 34% of Gen X consumers say they seek out foods and beverages that are good for their gut health.[10] This interest has fueled the growth of probiotic and prebiotic foods and supplements, with the global probiotics market expected to reach $77.09 billion by 2025.

Gen X's interest in gut health extends beyond probiotics. Fermented foods such as kombucha, kefir, and kimchi have seen a surge in popularity. The kombucha market, for instance, is projected to grow at a CAGR of 23.2% from 2019 to 2027, with Gen X being a key consumer demographic.[11]

It's hard to talk about gut health without mentioning the other g-word: gluten. Gen X has witnessed a significant rise in awareness and diagnosis of gluten-related disorders, such as celiac disease and non-celiac gluten sensitivity. Many in this generation have adopted gluten-free diets either out of necessity due to medical conditions or as a lifestyle choice, believing it contributes to better overall health. This shift has been driven in part by greater access to information and advancements in medical diagnostics.

The gluten-free diet trend gained substantial momentum during the 2000s when many Gen Xers were in their prime adult years. This generation has been instrumental in fueling the demand for gluten-free products, leading to a market explosion in gluten-free alternatives. These products, which were once scarce and often unappetizing, are now widely available and varied, ranging from breads and pastas to beers, snacks, and desserts.

For businesses, Gen X's focus on nutrition and gut health in particular provides a wealth of opportunities. Personalized nutrition services, functional foods targeting specific health concerns, and gut health-focused products are all areas ripe for innovation. Additionally, there's a growing demand for educational content and coaching services to help Gen Xers navigate the complex world of nutrition science. Give them the science-based guidance they're seeking, and they'll eat right out of your hand.

A Weighty Gen X Subject

There are volumes now dedicated to the prescription drugs that are dominating health-care and weight-loss headlines.

Originally formulated to treat diabetes, Ozempic, Mounjaro, Wegovy, and others have become a staple of weight management. While not limited to use by Gen Xers, these drugs are especially appealing to them, as many are beginning to experience slowing metabolisms and are having a harder time managing body weight.

Many Gen X celebs—Kelly Clarkson, Amy Schumer, Tracy Morgan, to name a few—have served as high-profile influencers for the weight-loss drugs. The massive expansion of these drugs has been disruptive to traditional weight-loss programs such as Weight Watchers (rebranded as WW). At the same time, it has sparked research for their application, potentially rendering some businesses obsolete while creating new opportunities for growth. Businesses and investors are wise to keep their eyes on this dynamic category and how it will impact Gen X.

Skin Health and Protection

For Generation X, skin care is no longer just about looking good; it's also about overall skin health, protection, and maintaining a youthful appearance as they navigate their 40s and 50s. This generation grew up during the tanning bed craze of the 1980s and early 1990s, and now they're dealing with the consequences while trying to prevent further damage.

According to the American Academy of Dermatology, adults aged 40 to 60 are the fastest-growing demographic for dermatological procedures, with a 32% increase in treatments over the past five years.[12] This surge reflects Gen Xers' proactive approach to skin care and their willingness to invest in their appearance.

Key skin-care trends among Gen X include the following:

- Antiaging Treatments: Gen X is driving growth in the antiaging skin-care market. The global antiaging market is expected to reach $119.6 billion by 2030, with Gen X as a key consumer group.[13] Popular treatments include retinoids, peptides, and antioxidants, all of which are designed to replenish the elements that skin naturally loses over time.

- Noninvasive Procedures: While Gen Xers are open to cosmetic procedures, they tend to prefer less invasive options. The American Society for Dermatologic Surgery reports that Gen X patients most commonly request treatments such as Botox, dermal fillers, and chemical peels. Dubbed "injectables," they are a less invasive alternative to facelifts that were the Boomers' antiaging go-to.

- Laser Treatments: Laser treatments have become a popular choice among Gen Xers to battle sun damage and aging. Techniques such as fractional laser treatments, intense pulsed light (IPL), and nonablative laser procedures are particularly sought after for their ability to reduce pigmentation, improve skin texture, and stimulate collagen production without extensive downtime. These procedures are appealing to a generation that values effective, minimally invasive solutions.

For Gen X, skin care is not just about repair but also about prevention and maintaining a youthful appearance. Laser treatments offer a dual benefit: They correct existing damage and help to rejuvenate the skin, making it look fresher and more youthful. This aligns with Gen X's broader interest in antiaging strategies, which often include a combination of skin-care products, treatments, and lifestyle choices.

> **"I grew up spending my summers at the swimming pool using baby oil to intensify my tan. I had no idea about long-term sun damage. Now every teenage sunburn is showing up on me as an age spot."**
>
> —GEN X MOM, AGE 54

In general, the technological advancements in laser technology and facial "injectables" have made these treatments safer, more effective, and more accessible, which has contributed to their popularity among Gen Xers. The ability to target specific skin issues with precision and the reduced risk of side effects compared with earlier methods have made cosmetic treatments a preferred option for many in this generation.

As we've seen, Gen Xers tend to be informed consumers who research and carefully consider the benefits and risks—and that is definitely true of cosmetic procedures. Many choose treatments not just for aesthetic reasons but also as part of a broader commitment to maintaining healthy skin. This generation is more likely to consult with dermatologists and skin-care professionals to ensure that the treatments they undergo are safe and effective.

> "I'm outside for my job, and skin cancer runs in my family. I have my dermatologist check me every six months and remove any questionable growths or bumps. And I wear sunscreen. Skin health is a priority."
>
> —GEN X CONSTRUCTION WORKER, AGE 48

As Gen X continues to prioritize skin health and protection, they're looking for solutions that are effective, scientifically proven, and can keep them looking as young as they feel. Companies that can provide these solutions while educating consumers about the importance of long-term skin health are likely to find success with this image-conscious yet health-focused generation.

Mental Wellness and Stress Management

Generation X is increasingly recognizing the importance of mental health and stress management as crucial components of overall wellness. Having come of age during a time when mental health was often stigmatized, Gen Xers are now at the forefront of destigmatizing mental health care and prioritizing emotional well-being for themselves and their families.

According to a 2023 survey by the American Psychological Association, 47% of Gen X respondents reported wanting to seek mental health treatment in the past year.[14] This openness to addressing mental health issues is driving several trends:

- Mindfulness and Meditation: Gen X is embracing mindfulness practices as a way to manage stress and improve mental well-being. Meditation practice among adults aged 45 to 64 increased from 9.4% in 2012 to 15.9% in 2022.[15] This has fueled growth in meditation apps, mindfulness workshops, and wellness retreats.

- Work-Life Balance: As the generation that pioneered the concept of work-life balance, Gen X continues to prioritize this aspect of mental health. A survey by FlexJobs found that 81% of Gen X respondents cited work-life balance as the most important factor in evaluating a job prospect.[16] (This is despite their documented behavior of overworking after they accept a position.) As mentioned in Chapter 6, offering balance has big implications for employers and has driven the growth of flexible work arrangements and wellness programs.

- Therapy and Counseling: Gen Xers are more open to seeking professional mental health support than members of previous generations. The National Alliance on Mental Illness reports that Gen X has the highest rate of therapy utilization among all age groups. This includes traditional in-person therapy as well as online counseling platforms.

Surprised? Online therapy platforms such as BetterHelp and Talkspace have gained popularity and expanded access to therapy.

- Stress Reduction Techniques: With many Gen Xers juggling careers and family responsibilities along with caring for aging parents, stress management is a top priority. Popular stress-reduction techniques include yoga, breathwork, digital detox, and nature therapy. A study by the Global Wellness Institute found that the wellness tourism market, which includes stress-reduction retreats, is expected to reach $919 billion by 2025, with Gen X as a key demographic.

- Sleep Health: Gen X is increasingly recognizing the importance of sleep for mental health. Currently, 42% of Gen X adults use sleep tracking devices or apps, reflecting a growing interest in optimizing sleep quality.[17] There is no shortage of information, devices, or supplements that promise solutions for a better night's sleep. Gen Xer Arianna Huffington, the sleep evangelist, made getting a good night's sleep a national topic.

The Sober Curious Movement

The "sober curious" movement, characterized by a mindful approach to alcohol consumption or abstinence, has gained significant traction among Gen Xers as part of their expanding wellness quest. This trend reflects a growing awareness of the health impacts of alcohol and a desire for healthier lifestyle choices. Weight control, better sleep, and steadier mental health are three of the reasons often cited for adopting this practice.

According to a survey by Nielsen, 47% of US consumers aged 21 and older are making efforts to reduce their alcohol consumption.[18] Gen X, in particular, is driving this trend, with many reassessing their relationship with alcohol as they prioritize health and wellness in midlife.

The rise of the sober curious movement has led to a boom in the nonalcoholic beverage market. The global nonalcoholic beer market is expected to reach $23 billion by 2025, growing at a CAGR of 7.5%.[19] Innovative products such as alcohol-free spirits and sophisticated mocktails are also gaining popularity, catering to those who want the social experience of drinking *without* the alcohol. It has also led to a boom of apps to help with the sober curious transition. Kin Euphorics, Recess, and Peak Cocktails are a few of the brands in this space.

As Gen Xers continue to prioritize mental health and stress management, they're looking for solutions that are effective, scientifically backed, and easily integrated into their busy lives. Companies that can provide these solutions while helping to destigmatize mental health care are likely to find success with this emotionally aware generation.

Personalized and Preventative Medicine

Gen X is spearheading a paradigm shift in health care, moving from reactive treatment to proactive prevention and personalization.

As technology pioneers, Gen Xers are embracing strategies to control their health and make informed care decisions. This generation is set to radically depart from the health-care systems and primary doctor supervision they grew up with.

Genetic testing has gained popularity among Gen Xers, with companies like 23andMe and AncestryDNA seeing significant growth. These tests provide insights into genetic health risks, enabling preventative measures. The global genetic testing market is expected to reach $28.5 billion by 2026, driven by consumer interest in health-related genetic information.[20] Our cultural love affair with genetics is no longer just Boomer grandmothers sitting at their computers, sipping a cup of chamomile while poring over their family trees.

Personalized health plans based on genetics and individual data are gaining traction, offering tailored recommendations for diet, exercise, and preventative screenings. A 2018 Accenture survey found that 83% of consumers are willing to share their health data for personalized care.

Health-conscious Gen Xers prioritize preventative screenings and early detection, often seeking screenings earlier than traditionally recommended. They've also rapidly adopted telemedicine and digital health tools, valuing convenience and technological comfort. A Rock Health survey found that 43% of Gen X respondents had used telemedicine services.[21]

Personalized medicine represents the next frontier. By addressing Gen X's desire for tailored health-care solutions, businesses can position themselves as valuable partners in this generation's quest for optimal health and longevity. In a tech-enabled environment where treatments can be customized to individual DNA, Gen X is poised to demand these advanced services.

Wellness Below the Belt

Does the conversation make you uncomfortable? There are some highly targeted Gen X wellness topics that businesses did not talk about "in nice company" years ago. But with a pragmatic, matter-of-fact approach, important topics and solutions are busting through on all media, loud and proud—menopause, perimenopause, erectile dysfunction, vaginal dryness, and manscaping, to name a few. The shift? Fewer topics are taboo, and advertisers can more effectively focus their media on targeted audiences.

There are a couple of companies that are doing this well. Revaree is a product to treat vaginal dryness that commonly occurs in women 50 and older. Revaree uses influencers, specifically well-known female doctors, to explain the product and the science in Instagram video ads. It's a well-targeted go-to-market strategy to sell Revaree subscriptions.

Evernow provides menopause support services and telehealth, with access to hormone replacement therapy and nonhormonal solutions. Their solutions address the gamut of symptoms that can accompany menopause, ranging from hot flashes and sleep disruption to depression, weight gain, and thinning hair. What seems to work for Gen X is an evidence-based approach along with digital and human solutions. There are several up-and-comers in this space—businesses such as Midi Health and Winona, as well as telehealth services such as Alloy. Interestingly, more companies are now adding menopause benefits to their health plans to meet the needs of their Gen X employees.

Clearly, we have moved beyond the oh-so-subtle "two bathtubs" Cialis commercial when it comes to Gen Xers' sexual and life-stage health. Companies and investors should utilize the principles we've outlined in this book to deliver solutions to this audience and campaigns that resonate.

Conclusion: The Gen X Wellness Opportunity

Generation X's approach to wellness represents a significant shift in how midlife health is perceived and pursued. This generation, now in their 40s and 50s, is redefining what it means to age well, embracing a holistic approach that encompasses physical fitness, nutrition, skin care, mental health, and preventative medicine.

For businesses, the Gen X wellness market presents a deep well of opportunities. This generation's willingness to invest in their health, coupled with their tech savviness and desire for personalized solutions, creates a perfect storm for innovative wellness products and services. From fitness tech to personalized nutrition plans, from advanced skin-care treatments to mental health apps, the possibilities are vast and varied.

However, capturing the Gen X wellness market requires more than just offering products or services. It demands a deep understanding of this generation's unique needs, values, and life-stage challenges. Gen Xers value authenticity, scientific backing, and solutions that fit seamlessly into their busy lives. They're not looking for quick fixes or miracle cures but rather sustainable, evidence-based approaches to maintaining their health and vitality. The future of wellness for Gen Xers is not just about living longer; it's also about living well. That's a religion they can get behind.

X FACTOR TAKEAWAYS
Growing Revenue with Gen X Wellness

- **Address Holistic Wellness:** Recognize that for Gen Xers, wellness isn't just about physical health. Offer solutions that address mental, emotional, and even spiritual well-being alongside physical health, acknowledging the interconnectedness of these aspects.

- **Make It Personal:** Gen Xers seek tailored wellness solutions. Invest in technologies and services that allow for customization based on individual needs, from genetic testing to personalized fitness, skin treatments, and nutrition plans.

- **Balance Technology with a Human Touch:** While Gen X appreciates tech-enabled wellness solutions, they also value expert guidance. Offer digital tools but ensure there's personal interaction or professional support available when needed. Apps and trackers are good, but providing a live-coach option is fantastic.

- **Focus on Prevention and Optimization:** Position your products or services as tools for maintaining health and enhancing quality of life. Gen Xers are interested in preventative measures and optimizing their well-being, not just treating problems. No judgment about cosmetic procedures or products to extend a youthful appearance or lifestyle—that's part of the new wellness approach.

- **Provide Education and Transparency:** Gen Xers value knowledge and authenticity. Offer clear, science-based information about your products or services, and be transparent about their benefits and limitations.

CHAPTER 9

Gen Xers Living Their Best Lives

"I Wanna Dance with Somebody (Who Loves Me)"
—Whitney Houston (1987)

As Whitney Houston's iconic voice blasted through boom boxes and car stereos in the late '80s, proclaiming her desire to dance with somebody, little did we know that those Gen X teenagers would grow up to be the ones setting the dance floor on fire—metaphorically speaking, of course. Now in their 40s and 50s, Gen Xers aren't just dancing; they're leading the conga line in a variety of markets, from luxury travel to high-end fashion.

While marketers have been busy trying to decode the enigma that is Gen Z, they're overlooking a gold mine hiding in plain sight. Gen Xers, with their substantial spending power and discerning tastes, are living their best lives and aren't afraid to shell out for quality experiences and products.

It's time for businesses to start obsessing about Gen X and asking, "Is that somebody who loves me?"

The Luxury Travel Boom: Gen X Takes Flight

Remember when a vacation meant piling into the family station wagon for a road trip to the nearest beach? Gen Xers sure do, and they're making up for lost time with a vengeance. This generation is leading the charge in luxury travel, seeking out unique high-end experiences that are a far cry from those budget motels of their youth.

According to a 2023 study by Luxury Travel Advisor, Gen Xers are spending more on luxury trips than any other age group. They're not just traveling more; they're also traveling better (the same study noted that 80% of luxury leisure spending is done by travelers aged 40 to 60).[1] Five-star hotels, exclusive resorts, and bespoke travel experiences are all on the menu for this generation of discerning globetrotters. They did their backpacking across Europe on a shoestring budget years ago. Now they want to see the world again, but with a good night's sleep and a spa treatment at the end of the day.

Gen Xers' travel preferences are shaped by their desire for authenticity, comfort, and unique experiences. They're less interested in cookie-cutter package tours and more drawn to personalized itineraries that offer a deep dive into local culture. This has led to a boom in experiential travel, with Gen Xers seeking out everything from culinary tours in Tuscany to wildlife safaris in Tanzania. They are also prioritizing trips that require endurance and fitness: Machu Picchu. The Great Wall of China. Glacier Park's Highline Trail. "Let's do it now while we're able" is the prevailing sentiment.

The travel industry would do well to cater to Gen Xers' specific needs and desires. They are driving the top end of this market. This means brushing up on your Gen X bucket list trips and figuring out the most unforgettable way to show them the Northern Lights. It also means offering a blend of adventure and comfort, incorporating technology without making it the focal point, and providing opportunities for meaningful connections and experiences.

This customer may be the one footing the bill for a whole family adventure at an all-inclusive in the islands. But unless it's *their* kids or grandkids, don't put them in a mid-market, family-friendly situation. They want the trip they can now afford.

Fashion Forward: Gen X's Love Affair with Luxury Brands

While Millennials and Gen Zers might be making headlines with their streetwear obsessions, Gen Xers are quietly dominating the luxury fashion market. Remember those flannel shirts and ripped jeans they used to wear? Well, they've been replaced by Gucci loafers and Chanel handbags.

A 2023 report by Bain & Company revealed that Gen X accounts for 40% of all luxury fashion purchases, more than any other generation. Brands like Gucci, Louis Vuitton, and Prada have seen a significant uptick in Gen X customers over the past five years.[2]

What's driving this luxury fashion boom among Gen Xers? For one, they have the disposable income to invest in timeless, high-quality pieces. But it's more than just having deep pockets. Gen Xers appreciate craftsmanship and heritage, values that align well with luxury brands. They're not chasing trends; they're investing in style.

Interestingly, Gen X's approach to luxury fashion is influencing younger generations. The resale market for luxury goods has exploded, with platforms such as The RealReal reporting that Gen X sellers are their biggest suppliers of authenticated luxury items.

It's not just the luxury brands; it's also the retailers that know how to make great fashion easy for Gen X, who are reaping the benefits. Nordstrom's free personal shoppers? Yes, thank you! Stitch Fix's personalized outfits sent to the home? Tech + fashion + convenience = yes, again. These Human-Digital experiences are a win. M.M.LaFleur is another retailer that does not apologize for its prices but has a frictionless digital shopping experience for classic workwear pieces.

> "Gen X customers are our sweet spot. They have the means to buy new luxury items, the confidence to wear them, and the savvy to resell them when they're ready for something new. It's a perfect cycle."
>
> —CMO, LUXURY RESALE PLATFORM

Luxury brands are starting to take notice of Gen X's purchasing power. We're seeing more age-diverse marketing campaigns and products that cater to Gen X's desire for both style and comfort. The message is clear: luxury isn't simply for the young or the old; it's for those who appreciate it, regardless of age.

Home Sweet Home: Gen X's Real Estate Renaissance

While Millennials have been dubbed "Generation Rent," Gen Xers are busy reshaping the luxury real estate market. With their peak earning years coinciding with a desire for space and comfort, Gen Xers are driving demand for high-end homes and second properties.

The National Association of Realtors reports that Gen X buyers account for 35% of luxury home purchases (properties defined as the top 5% of any given market). What's more, they're not just buying; they're also renovating and upgrading.[3]

> "I've waited 20 years to have a kitchen with a massive island and a wine fridge. Now that the kids are older, it's time to create the home I've always dreamed of."
>
> —GEN X HOMEOWNER, AGE 55

Gen Xers' approach to homeownership reflects their values and life stage. They're looking for spaces that can accommodate multigenerational living (remember, they're the sandwich generation), home offices for their evolving careers, and amenities that support their wellness goals.

The pandemic has only accelerated these trends. With more time spent at home, Gen Xers have been investing heavily in their living spaces. Home gyms, gourmet kitchens, and outdoor entertainment areas have all seen a surge in popularity among this cohort.

High-end appliance manufacturers are seeing a surge in Gen X customers. Sub-Zero and Wolf, known for their luxury refrigerators and ranges, reported in 2023 that Gen X now makes up 38% of their customer base, up from 25% just five years ago.

> **"Gen X customers come to us looking for restaurant-quality appliances for their home kitchens. They're not just cooking; they're creating culinary experiences for their families and friends."**
>
> —MARKETING DIRECTOR OF SUB-ZERO

The furniture and trappings have come along for the home upgrade ride. A Gen X breadwinner would prefer to work from a Herman Miller ergonomic chair in his or her home office. Both Crate & Barrel and Room & Board contain ampersands, yes—but they also both cater to the Gen X market, which can afford their luxury-for-the-masses product lines. For the high-end segment of these home goods categories, Gen Xers are the drivers.

The luxury and expectations don't end at the doormat. It may come as no surprise that Gen Xers, as the largest segment of homeowners, are also the heaviest investors in landscaping. Landscaping insiders tell us the asks for landscape designs include high-end hardscapes, outdoor kitchens, outdoor TVs, firepits, pizza ovens, eating areas, lounging areas, premium decking, pergolas, and Jacuzzis. Depending on the size of the yard, the plantings, and the materials, it's easy for these landscaping projects to hit six figures.

But the ideal outdoor setting is what they have been dreaming of, and if possible, a Gen Xer will invest in a space to host family get-togethers and create memories that will last forever.

Real estate developers and home improvement brands have a significant opportunity to cater to Gen X's home aspirations. This means offering products and services that blend functionality with luxury and understanding that for Gen X, a home is more than just a place to live; it's also a reflection of their journey and a canvas for their future.

Tech-Savvy and Loving It: Gen X's Digital Upgrade

As we have established, Gen Xers aren't technologically challenged; they're tech enthusiasts with discerning tastes and the means to indulge them. The generation that came of age during the personal computer revolution is now at the forefront of adopting high-end tech products and services.

A 2023 report by Deloitte found that Gen X outspends all other generations on personal technology, with an average annual spend of $3,200 per household.[4] From the latest smartphones to smart home systems, Gen X is all in on the digital revolution.

> ## "I have a smart home system that would make the Jetsons jealous."
>
> —GEN X TECH ENTHUSIAST, AGE 50

What sets Gen Xers apart in the tech market is their willingness to invest in quality and their appreciation for devices that seamlessly blend into their lives. They're less likely to chase the latest fad and more interested in technology that offers tangible benefits.

This preference is evident in the success of high-end audio equipment among Gen Xers. Brands such as Bose and Sonos have seen significant growth in this demographic, with Gen X audiophiles willing to spend top dollar for premium sound quality.

The smart home trend is also fueled by tech-savvy Gen X homeowners. What started with Alexa has now evolved to encompass brands and products like smart lighting, including Philips Hue's and LIFX's LED lightbulbs that can be controlled by smartphone apps; smart thermostats, including the Nest and Ecobee brands; and smart home security systems, including the one made by Ring.

Another area where Gen X is making significant tech investments is in advanced home entertainment systems. The pandemic accelerated this trend, with many Gen Xers upgrading their home theaters to recreate the cinema experience. Gen X households are 35% more likely than those of other generations to own a 4K or 8K TV, and they are 40% more likely to have a dedicated home theater room.[5]

This investment in home entertainment technology aligns perfectly with Gen Xers' life stage. With many in this generation having older children or empty nests, they have both the space and the disposable income to create these high-end entertainment spaces. And circling back to the family-time theme, creating spaces for shared entertainment ranks high with this demographic.

We discussed how Gen Xers are gamers. Well, that insight shows up at the proverbial cash register. The gaming industry has seen a surge in Gen Xers' interest in the realm of virtual reality (VR) and augmented reality (AR). While these technologies are often associated with younger generations, a 2023 report from SuperData Research revealed that Gen X makes up 28% of VR users and spends on average 20% more on VR hardware and software than other age groups.[6]

The opportunity for tech companies is clear: Create products that offer sophistication, quality, and utility. Gen Xers don't need to be dazzled by flashy features; they want technology that enhances their lives in meaningful ways, whether it's through superior audio experiences, immersive home entertainment, or cutting-edge gaming technology.

Luxury Wellness: Gen X Goes Premium

As we just established in Chapter 8, Gen Xers aren't slowing down; they're doubling down on health and wellness. Gen X accounts for 45% of all spending in the premium wellness sector, including high-end gym memberships, personal training services, and wellness retreats.[7]

The fitness industry has seen a shift in catering to an upscale Gen X. Boutique fitness studios offering personalized, low-impact workouts have gained popularity. Luxury gym chains have also seen a surge in Gen X memberships. Equinox, known for its high-end facilities and premium pricing, reported in 2023 that Gen X members make up 42% of their membership base despite the hefty annual fees that can range from $2,200 to $26,000 for their most exclusive tiers.[8]

"Our Gen X members are our most loyal. They appreciate the quality of our facilities, the expertise of our trainers, and the comprehensive wellness approach we offer. They're not just here for a workout; they're investing in their overall well-being."

—EQUINOX MEMBERSHIP MANAGER

Another area where Gen X is making significant wellness investments is in recovery and regenerative therapies. Cryotherapy chambers, infrared saunas, and hyperbaric oxygen therapy sessions—once the domain of professional athletes—are now being embraced by Gen X wellness aficionados.

The trend extends beyond gym walls to luxury fitness retreats. Gen X travelers account for 53% of all bookings for premium fitness and wellness retreats.[9] These aren't your average yoga getaways; we're talking about high-end experiences that combine intense physical activities with luxury accommodations and gourmet, health-focused cuisine. For many busy and stressed Gen Xers, a week at a fitness retreat is the perfect vacation. If they can afford the splurge, they report that the experience recharges them physically and mentally. And, going back to the "fitness is a team sport" theme, it puts them in a community of like-minded people who share wellness values.

From luxury gym memberships and high-end fitness retreats to cutting-edge recovery therapies, Gen Xers are proving that when it comes to wellness, they're willing to invest in quality experiences that deliver results.

Epicurean Adventures: Gen X's Culinary Quest

Move over, foodie Millennials. Despite all the wisecracks about their beloved avocado toast, it's actually Gen X that's taking center stage in the culinary world. With refined palates and the means to indulge them, this generation is driving growth in the gourmet food and beverage market.

A 2023 report by the National Restaurant Association found that Gen X diners spend an average of 25% more per meal at high-end restaurants than diners of other generations. They're not just eating out more; they're also pursuing unique, elevated dining experiences.

This culinary enthusiasm extends to the home kitchen as well. Gen X has been a driving force behind the growth of gourmet cooking stores and high-end kitchen appliances. Williams-Sonoma reported in their 2023 Annual Report that Gen X customers accounted for 42% of their sales in the premium cookware category.[10]

The wine and spirits industry has also seen significant Gen X influence. This generation is more likely to splurge on premium bottles and is driving growth in the craft spirits market. According to the Wine Market Council, Gen X consumers are more likely than any other generation to spend more than $50 on a bottle of wine.[11]

This trend extends to the booming craft spirits market as well. In 2023, Gen X consumers accounted for 45% of all premium craft spirit sales, outspending both Millennials and Baby Boomers in this category.[12] Looks like the takeaway is that the not "sober curious" Gen Xers are more likely to be premium booze consumers.

> ## "It's true. Life's too short for bad food."
> —GEN XER FROM SAN FRANCISCO, AGE 49

Much like in the food scene, the Gen X presence is driving the at-home coffee economy. From Nespresso machines to high-end La Marzocco espresso machines, Gen Xers are investing in authentic gourmet experiences in their daily lives.

For food and beverage brands, the opportunity lies in offering products and experiences that cater to Gen Xers' sophisticated palates and desire for quality. This could mean everything from gourmet meal kit services to exclusive wine clubs and chef-led cooking classes.

One such success story is the rise of high-end meal kit services tailored for Gen X consumers. Blue Apron, for instance, launched a premium line in 2022, targeting Gen X with restaurant-quality ingredients and chef-designed recipes.

Within a year, this premium line accounted for 35% of the company's total revenue, with 80% of subscribers falling into the Gen X demographic.[13]

> "Our Gen X subscribers don't just want convenience; they want an elevated home-cooking experience. They want premium ingredients and innovative recipes."
>
> —BLUE APRON MARKETER

From fine dining and premium home cooking to craft spirits and specialty coffees, Gen X is driving the trend toward higher quality, more sophisticated culinary experiences. For brands in the food and beverage industry, catering to Gen Xers' tastes and willingness to invest in quality presents a significant opportunity for growth in the premium market segment.

Passion Projects: Gen X's Renaissance of Personal Pursuits

As Gen Xers enter their prime years, they're not just focusing on material success; they're also leaning into their passions and personal growth in ways that reflect their values and life experiences. This generation, known for its independence and adaptability, is now channeling these traits into meaningful pursuits that go beyond the professional realm.

One area in which Gen X is making a significant impact is in volunteerism and community engagement. According to a 2023 study by the Corporation for National and Community Service, Gen X has the highest volunteer rate of any generation, with 36% actively volunteering in their communities. Many are leveraging their professional skills to make a difference, whether it's via pro bono consulting for nonprofits or taking on leadership roles in local organizations. This surge in civic engagement isn't just about giving back; it's also about Gen Xers finding purpose and connection in their communities.

Spiritual and personal growth pursuits are also gaining traction among Gen Xers. Beyond yoga studios and meditation retreats, personal development workshops are seeing an influx of Gen X participants. A 2023 survey by the Pew Research Center found that 42% of Gen Xers consider themselves "spiritual but not religious," the highest percentage of any generation. This has led to a boom in alternative spiritual practices and self-discovery programs tailored to this demographic. From silent retreats to ayahuasca ceremonies, Gen Xers are exploring paths to inner peace and self-understanding with the same curiosity and intensity they once applied to their careers.

Family time, too, has taken on new significance for many Gen Xers. As their children grow older or leave the nest, many are redefining family relationships and creating new traditions. Travel companies report a surge in multigenerational trips booked by Gen X clients, reflecting a desire to create lasting memories with both aging parents and growing children. At the same time, some are discovering the joys of grandparenthood, with "glam-mas" and "grand-dudes" rewriting the rules of what it means to be a grandparent in the 21st century.

Lastly, Gen X is embracing new hobbies and skills with gusto. From baking artisanal bread and crafting pottery to learning a new language, this generation is proving that it's never too late to pick up a new passion. Platforms like Master-Class have a great opportunity with Gen Xers to grow their subscriber base. This pursuit of lifelong learning isn't simply about personal fulfillment; it's about Gen Xers staying relevant and engaged in a rapidly changing world.

Conclusion: The Gen X Factor

Generation X is far from being the forgotten middle child of demographics. Gen Xers are living their best lives, indulging in luxury travel, fashion, homes, technology, wellness, and culinary experiences. Their significant spending power, coupled with their discerning tastes, makes them a dream demographic for businesses across various sectors.

The key to tapping into the Gen X market is understanding their unique blend of values: Gen Xers appreciate quality and are willing to pay for it. They value authenticity and experiences over mere possessions. They're tech-savvy but not tech-obsessed. And perhaps most importantly, they're at a stage in life where they're prioritizing their own wants and needs, often for the first time.

> "I'm happily married, have two nice kids,
> drive an Audi convertible, and I'm wearing
> a Burberry coat. I think I've made it!"
>
> —YOUR ANNOYING GEN X BESTIE, AGE 48

For businesses, the message is clear: Ignore Gen X at your peril. While the allure of capturing the youth market is strong, the real spending power lies with this generation of former latchkey kids turned luxury consumers. Don't forget, it's often Gen Xers funding their kids' splurges, so their economic clout extends beyond them. It's time to turn up the Whitney Houston, hit the dance floor, and start courting the Gen X customer. After all, they've waited long enough to be the center of attention—and they have the credit cards to prove it.

Premium brands and services take note: While Gen Zers might be dancing on TikTok, Gen Xers are the ones signing the checks. It's time for businesses to shift their focus from asking "What do Gen Zers want?" to "How can we attract Gen Xers?" Because when it comes to spending power and market influence, Gen Xers are ready to dance with someone who loves them.

X FACTOR TAKEAWAYS
Helping Gen Xers Live Their Best Lives

- **Luxury Market Dominance:** Gen X is a powerhouse in the premium segment of several categories, from travel and fashion to real estate and gourmet experiences, with the spending power to match their discerning tastes.

- **Quality and Authenticity Seekers:** This generation values quality, authenticity, and meaningful experiences over mere possessions, making them ideal customers for high-end, well-crafted products and services.

- **Tech-Savvy Luxury Consumers:** Gen X's tech savviness, combined with their appreciation for functionality, positions them as key consumers in the premium technology and smart home markets.

- **Wellness Investors:** Wellness and self-care are priorities for Gen X, driving growth in holistic health services, fitness programs, and preventative care tailored to their life stage.

- **Untapped Market Potential:** Businesses across sectors have a significant opportunity to tap into Gen X's economic clout by understanding and catering to their specific needs, preferences, and values.

CHAPTER 10

Gen Xcellerators

"Everybody Wants to Rule the World"

—Tears for Fears (1985)

By now, we hope you'll agree there's an upside to engaging the Gen X audience, as well as considerable opportunity costs of missing out on this prime consumer segment. We've highlighted several companies doing an outstanding job connecting with Gen X and providing what they need.

But how much of the Gen X connection is a happy accident? How many companies have proactively made Gen X central to their growth strategies?

A few chapters back, we highlighted Adobe, Squarespace, and LegalZoom for offering much-needed services tailored to the needs of Gen X fractional and interim workers. But those business strategies and services were designed for *all* entrepreneurs, not just Gen Xers. The same is true for wellness companies such as Headspace, BetterHelp, and Noom: They all provide great mental health tools with digital interfaces and personalization features. But, again, these wellness services were designed for *everyone,* not specifically Gen Xers.

As marketers in the Gen X space, we make it our mission to proactively seek out the companies that are targeting Gen X to make this segment central to their growth strategies. We call these companies and brands **GEN XCELLERATORS**, as they help raise the bar for keeping Gen X optimally activated and engaged.

The question we pose to you is this: What can you and your business learn from these companies' strategies and solutions so that you, too, can expand your customer base and your revenues?

In this chapter, we'll use the lens of our three super categories—Work, Wealth, and Wellness—to identify a number of companies that are currently delivering on the key points we've shared. Some of them are iconic brands; others are smaller but making their mark. These companies have set themselves apart with their approach to Gen X, and they are reaping the benefits.

We know that everybody wants to rule the world—or at least their own business categories—so let's see who has scored a coveted spot on the **GEN XCELLERATORS LIST** and what they can teach us about how to Xcel.

Work—Gen Xcellerators

"How the world works" is a dynamic combination of employees and employers who productively align every day to generate value. This phrase was actually the first brand campaign for Indeed, the premier job search platform, back in 2014.[1] It's no less important today as we spotlight companies that are best in class in "how the Gen X world works."

In the realm of work, Gen Xcellerators are those companies that are getting ahead of demographic shifts, embracing age diversity, fostering new career trajectories, offering flexible work models, and facilitating the new entrepreneurial Gen X side hustle and fractional trends.

We previously highlighted L'Oréal and Allianz for their focus on retention and recruitment of employees aged 50 and above. But what about others who are meeting the key work dynamics of Gen X? Who are additional Xcellerators that will help change the Gen X work growth paradigm?

Deloitte, Salesforce, and UnitedHealthcare

These three giants stand out for their proactive approach to age diversity and flexible work models, particularly those that benefit Gen X employees. They are all distinct business models:

- Deloitte: A leading global provider of audit, consulting, tax, and advisory services

- Salesforce: A cloud-based software company in customer relationship management

- UnitedHealthcare: One of the largest health insurance providers in the United States

They all merit a mention, as each one is activating on three key Gen X work implications: age diversity, flexible work models, and tailored benefits.

Let's start by embracing age diversity. Each of these companies is recognized as an **age-friendly employer**, as they have signed the **AARP Employer Pledge Program**. This pledge signifies a company's commitment to hiring and retaining workers over 50 by creating an inclusive workplace and offering equal opportunities. Pro tip for Gen Xers: More than 1,000 companies have signed this pledge! If you are seeking new employment, this would be a useful research tool.

Deloitte and UnitedHealthcare also have robust initiatives and metrics. Deloitte has reported that Gen Xers make up 23% of its overall workforce and 74% of the partner, principal, and managing director (PPMD) roles. With that high concentration in key roles, it makes sense that they are focused on developing a multigenerational workforce, which can leverage this talent pool via employee research groups (ERGs) and leadership development of younger employees. We were excited to learn that UnitedHealthcare, a company focused on health and wellness, is now offering a menopause program with support and services geared toward their female Gen X employees. This is an innovative initiative we hope more companies will provide in the future.

Additionally, each of these companies offers benefits tailored to the Gen X challenges of being part of the sandwich generation, needing flexible work models, and requiring progressive health benefits. Programs include elder care assistance and tuition reimbursements, as well as deeper health screenings and other benefits. Part-time roles or remote work options are available for a variety of positions, allowing older workers to balance their professional and personal responsibilities. This flexibility is crucial for employees who require more manageable work schedules.

It is wonderful to see these large companies, with an average workforce ranging from 80,000 to 400,000 employees, expanding their programs and benefits for Gen Xers and more senior employees. Given their size and global brand recognition, they serve as benchmarks for all companies to adapt to changing workforce dynamics.

TrueBridge

So, what about those Gen Xers who are ready to leave traditional corporate life?

We've established that new work models, specifically fractional and interim roles, are growing quickly among Gen X. However, the challenge lies in connecting those in need of this talent with the talent seeking these opportunities.

Enter True, the global talent management platform dedicated to executive search excellence. In 2021, they established a fractional and interim placement arm called TrueBridge. This platform connects proven leaders with companies seeking interim executives or fractional leaders. Interim leaders are embedded in organizations, working full-time for a set period. Advisory or fractional leaders offer a consultative model, engaging for a limited number of hours per week or month to provide expert insight to a full-time executive or team.[2]

This work model favors Gen X for several reasons. True-Bridge placements have an average of 26 years of experience, must have previously held the role at another company, and boast a track record of results. Initial demand has arisen from smaller companies, usually private equity or venture capital-backed, that need immediate leadership or see value in getting a top performer to supercharge a function part-time.

Most Gen Xers interested in this type of work might be less excited or unsure where to find fractional or interim leads and marketing themselves. TrueBridge, as a well-respected executive recruiting firm, fills this gap by matching talent with opportunities. They can deliver a short list of targeted candidates to clients within days.

In 2024, Gen Xers with finance backgrounds accounted for the most placements, but TrueBridge reports a growing demand across marketing, human resources, engineering, and other fields. The future seems promising for leaders at the VP level and above to take on specific projects and roles. TrueBridge's rapidly evolving landscape exemplifies how companies can leverage changing demographics and benefit from seasoned talent. These Gen X hired guns might just open eyes to the value of experienced staffers!

> "The trend is the right talent for the right amount of time. Fractional or interim roles give seasoned executives the satisfaction and intensity of a full-time role while providing the opportunity to only work when it fits them. They still maintain the salary levels they're accustomed to, just prorated. It's a win-win for both the employer and the employee."
>
> —DAVID BEUERLEIN, FOUNDER, TRUEBRIDGE

TrueBridge makes the Gen Xcellerators list because they're bringing talent expertise and rigor to a new field in human resources and recruiting. As this practice grows, we expect that companies of all sizes will recognize the value of these work models in addressing demographic talent shifts and the need for more flexible employment. Leveraging the awareness and consideration that TrueBridge is driving is a winning strategy for Gen X.

X FACTOR TAKEAWAYS
Gen X Work

- **Prepare for Demographic Shifts:** Recognize the upcoming seismic shift in workforce demographics.

- **Embrace Age Diversity:** Implement strategies to attract, retain, and motivate Gen X workers (aged 45 to 60).

- **Redefine Career Trajectories:** Understand that Gen Xers may not follow traditional retirement paths. Develop strategies to accommodate fractional roles, consulting positions, or part-time/advisory roles.

- **Provide Flexible Work Models:** Offer diverse work arrangements, including remote work, mentoring roles, and paths to supporting their transition from side hustles to full-fledged businesses and boards.

- **Target Gen X Entrepreneurs:** Offer services and products for entrepreneurs and side hustlers. Gen Xers have the experience, financial means, and motivation to turn side gigs into sustainable businesses.

Wealth—Gen Xcellerators

The wealth management and advisory space is a key area where we would expect savvy companies to target Gen X. So, who makes the list in the wealth super category?

In the wealth management space, Gen Xcellerators are those companies providing informative and actionable content, offering diverse investment vehicles, planning for long-term wealth building, and delivering optimized Human-Digital experiences.

Atria Wealth Solutions

Atria Wealth Solutions, a part of LPL Financial, is a wealth management solutions holding company headquartered in New York. Atria supports approximately 2,400 advisors and 150 banks and credit unions, managing approximately $100 billion of brokerage and advisory assets. Established in 2017, Atria operates a network of broker-dealer subsidiaries focused on supporting independent financial advisors and institutions nationwide.[3]

Like other wealth management firms, it offers financial planning solutions, advisory technology, operational solutions, and practice management for the 2,400 advisors in their network. Atria is known for offering tools that help the advisors grow their practice and better serve clients. Atria is also one of the savvy firms that focused on the potential of Gen X.

CMO Bob Holcomb lays it out succinctly in the How We Think section of Atria's website. The key to an advisor's success is the Personalization Equation: "Know-What + Know-Who + Know-Why = Know-How."[4] While this equation is essential to all clients, we love that Atria calls out Gen X specifically.

Atria states that while Millennials and Gen Z might typically be called the NextGen growth opportunity, Gen X is actually the next generation poised for growth in wealth. Atria even created an Amplified Marketing Platform to help advisors target Gen X, using digital and face-to-face tools. Focusing on how to build trust with Gen X clients is a tenet. The goal is to make Gen X clients feel like the advisors "get" them, which results in the Gen Xers being more responsive to wealth-building ideas, as well as recommending the firm to their friends. Boom. We see this as a twofold growth Xcellerator move.

Fidelity Investments

We established early on in this book that while finances and wealth are complicated, Gen Xers are eager to become more educated. They are certainly adaptable, given the various economic cycles they have lived through, and as one of our experts said, they are the "figure it out" generation. To tackle the vast array of Gen Xers' needs, a company must commit to a robust content and media strategy backed by subject matter experts (SMEs). We believe financial industry giant Fidelity Investments is a standout.

Fidelity focuses on the broader Gen X market with accessible digital tools and significant educational content, which covers a range of investment strategies from basic to complex.

The company leverages technology to appeal to tech-savvy Gen Xers when outlining holistic financial solutions, wealth transfer information, and tailored retirement strategies. Interactive tools such as Full View®, the Client Lifetime Value Calculator, and the "Gen X Retirement Guide" allow users to track and manage investments. While self-directed engagement is prominent, Fidelity also offers access to financial advisors, which we know is key to the Gen X investor.

We especially appreciate Fidelity's media sophistication. The company blends traditional and digital media and utilizes webinars, podcasts, videos, and social media alongside events, TV ads, print ads, and direct mail. A perfect example is the monthly Insights Live[SM] events, which you can view online, but if you'd like a hard copy, you can download a PDF. But it's their staggering digital volume that sets them apart. According to their 2020 annual report, Fidelity had over 1.4 billion digital interactions on its retail mobile and web platforms alone, representing a 60% increase from 2019.[5] This includes blog posts, webinars, interactive tools, and videos tailored to different audiences, including Gen X. Even if you aren't a Fidelity customer, you can access their digital content, as it is all ungated (meaning you don't need to give them your name and email to access it). We know Gen X digital OGs crave information, and Fidelity delivers.

Lastly, Fidelity doesn't shy away from the good old compare and contrast. They are not afraid to list an age to discuss potential portfolios, etc. The following fictitious example of

Harry and Wendy Miller, aged 55 and planning to retire in 10 years, illustrates an everyday scenario that helps even novice Gen X investors gain valuable insights. It also includes guidance on how to connect to an expert for additional support. These offerings create that critical Human-Digital experience.

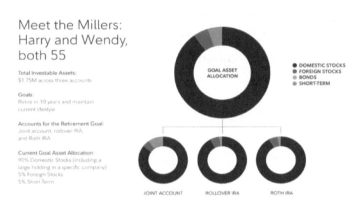

This is a hypothetical example and does not represent an actual client's portfolio.

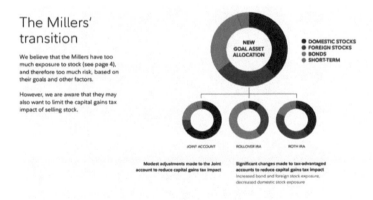

This is a hypothetical example and does not represent an actual client's portfolio.

Look, we recognize few companies have the scope and scale of Fidelity, with its more than 43 million client workplace accounts, $28 million in revenue, and servicing of 16,000 wealth management firms.[6] However, it is the fact that the company is making the effort to recognize what drives Gen X wealth that is so impressive. Today, brands of any size can create content, leverage innovative digital strategies, and develop interactive tools faster and more cost-effectively than ever before. Other wealth brands can take a page from Fidelity's explicit, or implied, Gen X go-to-market strategy and position themselves to win this cohort.

X FACTOR TAKEAWAYS
Gen X Wealth

- **Inform first and often. This is a prepared group.** Wealth building is complex, and Gen Xers are looking for informative content to guide them at every step. You can reach them via a variety of communication channels, but make sure they add value and are actionable.

- **Don't assume they aren't adaptable.** Gen Xers have seen the value of new business models and embraced investment vehicles outside of stocks and bonds, so be sure to talk to them about new opportunities.

- **Investing and wealth building don't stop at 50 or even 60.** Gen Xers are in their highest earning years and motivated to build. They might just want to invest in growth because they plan to live into their 80s and beyond!

- **Incorporate the Human-Digital experience.** Create a robust experience that uses the best digital features but allows for human interaction. Brands that make Gen Xers feel like they have personalized their wealth journey will win.

Wellness—Gen Xcellerators

We've touched on several companies, including Equinox, Revaree, and Evernow, that are showing up in this super category with effective Gen X go-to-market strategies. With such a broad category that ranges from fitness to nutrition, mental health, cosmetic procedures, and sexual health, it's hard to pick just a few for the wellness Gen Xcellerators list.

To be consistent with our criteria, we looked for the organizations that were delivering on the best practices of addressing Gen Xers' holistic wellness (beyond just physical fitness), personalizing services and products, delivering solutions with a Human-Digital experience, focusing on prevention and maintaining youthful vitality, and providing science-based education and information.

Hims, Juvéderm, and Mel Robbins

From the deep well of notable wellness Gen Xcellerators, we drew three unique businesses. They are distinctly different business models, but they all target and serve the Gen X market.

- Hims: Telehealth and products for Gen X men's hair loss and sexual health
- Juvéderm: Cosmetic filler treatments for Gen Xers' aesthetic procedures
- *The Mel Robbins Podcast*: Practical mindfulness targeted to Gen X listeners

Founded in 2017, Hims has positioned itself as a modern telehealth platform targeting men's health concerns that are particularly relevant to the Gen X demographic. Hims addresses issues such as hair loss, erectile dysfunction, and skin issues—topics that Gen X men may find uncomfortable discussing in traditional health-care settings. By offering online consultations and direct-to-consumer prescription delivery, Hims removes barriers to accessing care for these sensitive issues. This targeted focus on Gen Xers' health concerns, combined with a convenient and discreet service model, has allowed Hims to carve out a unique niche.

AbbVie is a global company offering innovative products and solutions that address complex health issues. One of these products is Juvéderm, an injectable filler aimed at Gen X consumers with a growing interest in noninvasive cosmetic procedures. This generation seeks ways to maintain a youthful appearance without surgery. Juvéderm's dermal fillers offer a quick, effective solution for reducing wrinkles and restoring volume, appealing to Gen Xers' desire for subtle, natural-looking results. The brand's marketing emphasizes confidence and self-care rather than vanity, aligning with Gen X values. By providing a range of products for different facial areas, Juvéderm allows for customized treatments, catering to the preference for personalized solutions in beauty and wellness routines.

The *Mel Robbins Podcast* makes the wellness grade for its contribution to Gen Xers' mental well-being. Mel delivers positivity and actionable hacks to living a happier life—especially for those Gen Xers living the sandwich generation reality. While she reminds listeners "I'm your friend, not your therapist," Mel's expert guests are legit neuroscientists, researchers, and psychologists. And her Midwestern midlife demeanor is simply good medicine for mental health. The best part? A digital podcast can be enjoyed anywhere. It's really the perfect Human-Digital service for Gen X.

Goop: Catering to Gen X's Holistic Wellness Needs

Founded by actress and Gen X icon Gwyneth Paltrow in 2008, Goop has emerged as a player in the wellness industry, successfully capturing the attention and loyalty of Gen X consumers.

Goop's success with Gen X can be largely attributed to its holistic approach to wellness. The brand recognizes that for this generation, wellness extends beyond physical health to encompass mental, emotional, and even spiritual well-being. The company offers a wide range of products and content addressing these interconnected aspects, from skin care and supplements to meditation guides and alternative healing practices.

Their wellness philosophy also aligns with Gen Xers' openness to cosmetic procedures and antiaging products as part of their overall wellness strategy. The brand offers a judgment-free space in which maintaining a youthful appearance is presented as a valid aspect of self-care and optimization.

Goop's success with Gen X is significantly bolstered by its robust digital direct-to-consumer strategy. Recognizing Gen X's comfort and proficiency with digital commerce, the company works through an online shopping experience that resonates with this tech-savvy generation. The brand's website serves as a central hub for both content and commerce, allowing Gen X consumers to transition from reading wellness articles to purchasing recommended products. This integrated approach capitalizes on Gen Xers' tendency to research before buying, providing them with the information they need and the convenient purchasing options they prefer. Goop's strong presence on social media platforms frequented by Gen X, such as Facebook and Instagram, allows for additional touchpoints and targeted advertising. This multichannel digital approach ensures that Goop remains accessible and relevant to Gen X consumers, meeting them where they already spend much of their time online.

While Goop leverages digital platforms for content delivery and e-commerce, it also recognizes Gen Xers' appreciation for expert guidance. The brand strikes a balance by offering tech-enabled solutions alongside access to wellness experts, doctors, and alternative practitioners through its content, events, and retreats.

It's worth noting, however, that Goop has faced criticism for some of its more controversial products and health claims. This underscores the importance of maintaining scientific rigor and transparency when targeting the well-informed and often skeptical Gen X audience. But despite its controversies, Goop's success in capturing a significant Gen X market share demonstrates the potential in addressing this generation's growing demand for holistic wellness solutions.

X FACTOR TAKEAWAYS
Gen X Wellness

- **Address Holistic Wellness:** Offer solutions that address mental, emotional, sexual, and even spiritual well-being alongside physical health.

- **Make It Personal:** Deliver technologies and services that allow for customization based on individual needs.

- **Balance Technology with a Human Touch:** Offer digital tools but ensure there's personal interaction or professional support available when needed.

- **Focus on Prevention and Optimization:** Position your products or services as tools for optimizing well-being and supporting youthful vitality.

- **Provide Education and Transparency:** Offer clear, science-based information about your products or services, and be transparent about their benefits and limitations.

Conclusion—Gen Xcellerators

The Gen Xcellerators we've explored demonstrate the potential of actively engaging with the Gen X segment in the Work, Wealth, and Wellness super categories. But the opportunities don't end there. By understanding and addressing the unique needs and preferences of this generation, companies can position themselves for growth and success.

X Factor impact means leaning into Gen X to grow revenue, market share, and bottom-line profits.

By implementing these strategies, companies across various sectors can tap into the significant potential of the Gen X market, driving growth and fostering long-term customer relationships with this influential generation. Does your company have the potential to grow your total addressable market and your revenue by focusing on this target? We help companies understand the path to becoming a Gen Xcellerator—because everybody wants to rule the world.

The Power of the Gen X Market

"The Power"

—Snap! (1990)

Unlocking the X Factor of Gen X Opportunity

In this book, we've explored the unique characteristics, experiences, and preferences that make Gen X a crucial target for businesses across various sectors. As the song says, "They've got the power." And now, so do you—the power to connect with this lucrative consumer segment.

The Gen X Paradigm Shift

We began by dispelling the myth of Gen X as the "forgotten generation." Born between 1965 and 1980, this cohort of approximately 65 million Americans controls an estimated $2.4 trillion in spending power. They are at the peak of their careers, often holding leadership positions, and possess significant purchasing power. Yet, despite their economic clout, Gen X remains underserved and under-targeted by many businesses.

Our exploration revealed a generation shaped by unique cultural and economic experiences. From being the first to grow up with personal computers to weathering multiple economic downturns, Gen Xers have developed a distinctive blend of tech savviness, pragmatism, and adaptability. These traits make them not just valuable consumers but also wealth builders and critical players in the workforce.

The Three Super Categories: Work, Wealth, and Wellness

Throughout this book, we've focused on three super categories that are particularly relevant to Gen X: **WORK**,

WEALTH, and **WELLNESS**. Let's recap the key insights in each area:

Work

Gen Xers are redefining the workplace as they progress through their 40s and 50s, evolving rather than slowing down. They are embracing flexible work models, including remote work and fractional roles, and are pioneering the gig economy while driving side hustle entrepreneurship. This generation values work-life balance without compromising high productivity, bringing valuable experience and leadership to organizations. Additionally, they provide crucial skill sets essential for navigating the seismic shifts occurring in the workforce.

Businesses that can adapt to Gen Xers' work preferences and leverage their experience will find a wealth of talent and expertise at their disposal.

Wealth

Gen Xers, currently in their prime earning years, are eager to keep investing and are well-positioned to benefit significantly from the great wealth transfer. They show a strong interest in diverse investment vehicles that go beyond traditional stocks and bonds, coupled with a desire for a blend of digital tools and human advisory services in wealth management. This generation prioritizes innovative long-term financial planning, particularly for retirement, while seeking education and transparency in financial products and services. They value portfolios that enable them to live fulfilling lives while still providing for their families.

Financial institutions and wealth management firms that can provide personalized, tech-enabled solutions while maintaining a human touch will be well-positioned to capture Gen X's growing wealth.

Wellness

Gen Xers are embracing a holistic approach to wellness that encompasses physical, mental, and emotional health. They are increasingly focused on preventative health measures and age-defying treatments, alongside a rising interest in personalized nutrition and fitness plans. This generation is also becoming more open to mental health services and stress management techniques, reflecting a growing awareness of the importance of emotional well-being. Additionally, they demonstrate a willingness to invest in premium wellness products and experiences that enhance their overall quality of life.

Companies in the health, fitness, and wellness sectors that provide tailored, science-backed solutions will find a highly receptive audience in Gen X.

The Gen X Opportunity: Turning Insights into Action

As we've demonstrated, Gen X represents a significant opportunity for businesses across various sectors. We call the companies that do it well "Gen Xcellerators." Capitalizing on this X Factor opportunity requires a nuanced understanding of Gen X's needs, preferences, and behaviors.

Here are some key strategies for ALL businesses looking to engage and win with Gen X:

- **Embrace the Human-Digital Experience:** Gen Xers appreciate the convenience of digital platforms that feel predictive and personal, and mimic the qualities of human interaction. Develop strategies that blend technology with dedicated service.

- **Prioritize Authenticity and Transparency:** Gen Xers are skeptical of marketing hype but accepting of marketing that delivers insights. Focus on providing clear, educational information about your products or services.

- **Offer Personalized Solutions:** Gen Xers value individualized experiences. Leverage data and technology to provide tailored products, services, and communications.

- **Recognize Their Life Stage:** Many Gen Xers are part of the sandwich generation, caring for both children and aging parents. Develop products and services that address these unique challenges.

- **Tap into Their Nostalgia:** While forward-thinking, Gen Xers also appreciate nostalgic references to their youth. Use this judiciously in your marketing efforts.

- **Provide Educational Content:** Gen X is a generation of lifelong learners. Offer valuable, informative content that helps Gen Xers make informed decisions.

- **Focus on Quality and Value:** Gen Xers are willing to spend on premium products and experiences but expect value for their money. Emphasize quality and long-term benefits in your offerings.

The Gen X Factor

And there you have it. Generation X, with all its strengths, tendencies, and quirks, represents a golden opportunity for businesses willing to invest in understanding and serving its members. From reshaping the workplace to driving growth in wealth management and wellness industries, Gen X is a force to be reckoned with.

The insights and strategies presented in this book provide a road map for businesses looking to tap into the Gen X market. By recognizing the unique characteristics of this generation and tailoring their approaches accordingly, companies can unlock significant growth potential and build lasting relationships with this influential cohort.

As authors and consultants, we are committed to helping businesses navigate the complexities of engaging with Gen X. We believe the companies that successfully harness this "X Factor" will be the ones who thrive in the coming decades.

The time to act is now. Gen Xers are in their prime, and their influence will only grow in the years to come. Will your business be ready to meet their needs and capture their loyalty? The opportunity is there; it's up to you to seize it. **You've got the power.**

Endnotes

Chapter 1: Who Is Gen X?

[1] Fid Backhouse. "Black Monday (1987) | Description & Facts." Encyclopedia Britannica, October 12, 2024. https://www.britannica.com/topic/Black-Monday-1987.

[2] Stern, Mark Joseph. "Why Are We So Nostalgic for Music We Loved as Teenagers?" *Slate* Magazine, August 13, 2014. https://slate.com/technology/2014/08/musical-nostalgia-the-psychology-and-neuroscience-for-song-preference-and-the-reminiscence-bump.html.

[3] Luminate (Formerly MRC Data). 2022 Year End Report.

[4] Pew Research Center Study, 2017.

[5] Graf, Nikki. "Today's Young Workers Are More Likely Than Ever to Have a Bachelor's Degree." Pew Research Center, April 14, 2024. https://www.pewresearch.org/short-reads/2017/05/16/todays-young-workers-are-more-likely-than-ever-to-have-a-bachelors-degree.

[6] "Digest of Education Statistics." U.S. National Center For Education Statistics. https://www2.census.gov/library/publications/2008/compendia/statab/128ed/tables/09s0292.pdf.

[7] National Center for Education Statistics. "Degrees Conferred by Postsecondary Institutions, by Level of Degree and Sex of Student: Selected Years, 1869-70 Through 2031-32." https://nces.ed.gov/programs/digest/d23/tables/dt23_318.10.asp.

[8] US Bureau of Labor Statistics.

[9] Nietzel, Michael T. "Women Continue to Outpace Men in College Enrollment and Graduation." *Forbes*, August 7, 2024. https://www.forbes.com/sites/michaeltnietzel/2024/08/07/women-continue-to-outpace-men-in-college-enrollment-and-graduation.

[10] FONA. "Consumer Insight: Generation X," April 26, 2023. https://www.mccormickfona.com/articles/2019/04/consumer-insight-generation-x.

[11] MetLife. "2024 Employee Benefit Trends Study." *MetLife*, March 18, 2024. https://www.metlife.com/workforce-insights/employee-benefit-trends/.

[12] Ibid

[13] Ibid

[14] https://www.cnbc.com/select/average-net-worth-by-age-40

[15] Mitchell, Travis, and Travis Mitchell. "1. Demographic and Economic Trends in Urban, Suburban and Rural Communities." Pew Research Center, April 14, 2024. https://www.pewresearch.org/social-trends/2018/05/22/demographic-and-economic-trends-in-urban-suburban-and-rural-communities.

[16] Katz, Lily, and Sheharyar Bokhari. "Gen Z's Homeownership Rate Stagnated in 2023, but Millennials and Gen Xers Saw Gains." Redfin Real Estate News, January 17, 2024. https://www.redfin.com/news/homeownership-rate-by-generation-2023.

[17] Bennett, Jesse, Kim Parker, and Amanda Barroso. "As Millennials Near 40, They're Approaching Family Life Differently Than Previous Generations." Pew Research Center, May 27, 2020. https://www.pewresearch.org/social-trends/2020/05/27/as-millennials-near-40-theyre-approaching-family-life-differently-than-previous-generations.

[18] "Generation Influence: Reaching Gen Z in the New Digital Paradigm." *WP Engine*.

[19] Statista. "Share of Amazon Shoppers in the United States 2023, by Generation," April 11, 2024. https://www.statista.com/statistics/1278936/amazon-shoppers-by-generation-united-states.

[20] "Insights | Merchant Solutions Insights | Worldpay." https://www.worldpay.com/en/insights/article/generation-pay-generation-x-spending-habits.

Chapter 2: The OG Digital Natives

[1] Pew Research Center, 2018.

[2] US Bureau of Labor Statistics, 1995.

[3] Educause, 2000.

[4] https://en.wikipedia.org/wiki/Personal_computer

[5] Hartley, Adam. "Laptop Sales Overtake Desktops." *TechRadar*, December 24, 2008. https://www.techradar.com/news/laptops/mobile-computing/computing/laptop-sales-overtake-desktops-497004.

[6] International Telecommunication Union, 2003.

[7] https://en.wikipedia.org/wiki/History_of_the_Internet

[8] "MarketResearch.com." https://www.marketresearch.com/IBISWorld-v2487/Web-Domain-Name-Sales-Research-35269489.

[9] Deloitte, 2010.

[10] Nielsen, 2012.

[11] Statista. "Number of MarTech Solutions Available Worldwide 2011-2024," May 16, 2024. https://www.statista.com/statistics/1131436/number-martech-solutions.

[12] Fraley, Amber. "Gen X Will Not Go Quietly." *Medium*, March 16, 2024. https://medium.com/kansas-genexstitential/gen-x-will-not-go-quietly-3b0429c63c70.

[13] "13 Stunning Stats on Gen X—the Forgotten-Yet-Powerful Generation." MONI Group. October 2018. https://www.monigroup.com/article/13-stunning-stats-gen-x-forgotten-yet-powerful-generation.

[14] The MTM Agency. "Social Media: Is Age Just a Number?," October 18, 2023. https://themtmagency.com/blog/the-generational-divide-on-social-media-is-age-really-just-a-number.

[15] Stone, Sorilbran. "2024 YouTube Audience Demographics: User Habits by Generation." The Shelf, a Data-First Influencer

Marketing Company, June 11, 2024. https://www.theshelf.com/
the-blog/youtube-user-habits.

[16] Lesonsky, Rieva. "How Do Different Generations Act on
Social Media?" SCORE. https://www.score.org/resource/
blog-post/how-do-different-generations-act-social-media.

[17] Roberts, Lauretta. "The Interview: Bobbi Brown,
Founder, JONES ROAD." TheIndustry.beauty,
October 21, 2022. https://theindustry.beauty/
the-interview-bobbi-brown-founder-jones-road.

[18] Fletcher Knight. "FK Insights: The Nuances of Targeting
Boomer Women." https://fletcherknight.com/fk-insights/
targeting-boomer-women.

[19] "Reality bytes: The digital experience is the human
experience." WP Engine. The Center for Generational Kinetics,
n.d. https://wpengine.com/wp-content/uploads/2019/01/
GenZ_RealityBytes_EbookEU.pdf.

[20] Brune, Mary. "Spotlight on: Gen X Gamers." Newzoo,
September 28, 2021. https://newzoo.com/resources/blog/
gen-x-gamers-how-gen-x-engage-with-video-games.

[21] Similarweb and Singular, 2024.

[22] Barna Group. "Hesitant & Hopeful: How Different
Generations View Artificial Intelligence - Barna Group," January
24, 2024. https://www.barna.com/research/generations-ai.

[23] Statista. "U.S.: Generative AI Adoption Rate in The
Workplace by Generation 2023 | Statista," December
11, 2023. https://www.statista.com/statistics/1361174/
generative-ai-adoption-rate-at-work-by-generation-us.

[24] Unite.ai, 2023.

[25] Ibid.

[26] Cykel.ai 2023.

[27] Charter, 2023.

[28] Accenture. "Reinvention in the Age of Generative AI," 2004.

Chapter 3: Money Matters

1 Williams, Ward. "Timeline of U.S. Stock Market Crashes."
Investopedia, October 30, 2024. https://www.investopedia.com/
timeline-of-stock-market-crashes-5217820.
2 Silver, Caleb. "Lessons From the 2008 Financial Crisis."
Investopedia, September 13, 2023. https://www.investopedia.
com/news/10-years-later-lessons-financial-crisis.
3 Tedeschi, Ernie. "Median Household Income by Birth Cohort
and Age Education-Adjusted." Edward Conard, December 12,
2018.
4 The Currency editors. "Financial Wisdom:
Top Money Moves by Generation." Empower.
https://www.empower.com/the-currency/life/
financial-wisdom-top-money-moves-by-generation.
5 "Generation X Workers' Retirement Collision Course Can
Still Be Corrected." Transamerica Center for Retirement Studies,
August 2014. https://www.transamericainstitute.org/research/
publications/details/generation-x-workers-retirement-collision-
course-can-still-be-corrected.
6 https://www.britannica.com/money/great-recession
7 Hoffower, Hillary, and Andy Kiersz. "Gen X Gained More
Wealth Than Any Generation During the Pandemic, Benefiting
From the Housing Boom and Their Peak Earning Years."
Business Insider, October 6, 2021. https://www.businessinsider.
com/gen-x-gained-most-wealth-during-pandemic-2021-10.
8 https://www.reuters.com/graphics/USA-ECONOMY/
GREATREBOOT
9 David, Patty, Gelfeld, Vicki, and Andreina Rangel. "Generation
X and Its Evolving Experience With the American Dream."
AARP, October 25, 2023. https://www.aarp.org/pri/topics/
aging-experience/demographics/genx-evolving-experience.
10 Currier, Erin. "How Generation X Could Change the
American Dream." The Pew Charitable Trusts, January 26,

2018. https://www.pewtrusts.org/en/trend/archive/winter-2018/how-generation-x-could-change-the-american-dream.
[11] Ibid

Chapter 4: The Sandwich Generation

[1] National Endowment for Financial Education, 2022.
[2] National Alliance for Caregiving and AARP study.
[3] "Median Cost of Nursing Home, Assisted Living, & Home Care | Genworth." https://www.genworth.com/aging-and-you/finances/cost-of-care/cost-of-care-trends-and-insights.
[4] Campbell-Dollaghan, Kelsey. "The Future of Housing Looks Nothing Like Today's." Fast Company, May 6, 2019. https://www.fastcompany.com/90342219/the-future-of-housing-looks-nothing-like-todays.
[5] National Alliance for Caregiving.
[6] National Center for Education Statistics.
[7] Richter, Felix. "Americans Owe $1.75 Trillion in Student Debt." Statista Daily Data, August 24, 2022. https://www.statista.com/chart/24477/outstanding-value-of-us-student-loans.
[8] National Association of Realtors.
[9] DeSilver, Drew. "For Most U.S. Workers, Real Wages Have Barely Budged in Decades." Pew Research Center, April 14, 2024. https://www.pewresearch.org/short-reads/2018/08/07/for-most-us-workers-real-wages-have-barely-budged-for-decades.
[10] Education Data Initiative, 2024.
[11] Forrest, Kim. "How Much Does the Average Wedding Cost, According to Data?" The Knot, August 22, 2024. https://www.theknot.com/content/average-wedding-cost.
[12] Kupriyanov, Volodymyr. "2023 Study: Insights Into the 26% of Americans in the Sandwich Generation." HireAHelper, September 27, 2023. https://blog.hireahelper.com/2023-study-insights-into-americans-in-the-sandwich-generation.

Chapter 5: The Midlife Categories That Count

[1] Syndio. "Workplace Equity by Generation: Baby Boomer, Gen X, Millennial & Gen Z Stats," November 16, 2022. https://synd.io/blog/workplace-equity-by-generation-stats-millennial-pay-gap.
[2] "The Fed - Distribution: Distribution of Household Wealth in the U.S. Since 1989." https://www.federalreserve.gov/releases/z1/dataviz/dfa/distribute/chart/.

Chapter 6: Work

[1] Peck, Emily. "Zoomers Will Overtake Boomers at Work Next Year." Axios, November 20, 2023. https://www.axios.com/2023/11/22/gen-z-boomers-work-census-data.
[2] Team, Prt Staffing Content. "The Changing Face of the Workforce: Gen X, Millennials, and Gen Z." PRT Staffing (blog), June 24, 2024. https://www.prtstaffing.com/news/the-changing-face-of-the-workforce-gen-x-millennials-and-gen-z.
[3] Greenwood, Shannon. "1. The Growth of the Older Workforce." Pew Research Center, April 14, 2024. https://www.pewresearch.org/social-trends/2023/12/14/the-growth-of-the-older-workforce.
[4] Berger, Chloe. "Meet the Typical Fortune 500 CEO: A Total Gen Xer. Basically Keanu Reeves." Fortune, June 8, 2023. https://fortune.com/2023/06/08/how-old-fortune-500-ceo-gen-x-keanu-reeves-musk.
[5] OECD (Organisation for Economic Co-operation and Development) and Generation study, 2023.
[6] Rockwood, Kate. "Hiring in the Age of Ageism." SHRM, December 21, 2023. https://www.shrm.org/topics-tools/news/hr-magazine/hiring-age-ageism.
[7] Shively, Brett. "How to Stop Ageism, Tech's Most Persistent Bias." Built In, December 19, 2023. https://builtin.com/articles/stop-ageism-tech.
[8] United States Bureau of Labor Statistics.

[9] Innes, Molly. "Almost Three Quarters of Marketers Aged Under 45, Study Finds." Marketing Week, February 7, 2023. https://www.marketingweek.com/marketing-skews-young-stats.

[10] Dan, Avi. "Is Ageism the Ugliest 'Ism' on Madison Avenue?" Forbes, September 15, 2016. https://www.forbes.com/sites/avidan/2016/09/13/is-ageism-the-ugliest-ism-on-madison-avenue.

[11] "Moody's ESG Solutions: ESG Profile 74/100." L'Oréal, March 13, 2023. https://www.loreal.com/en/news/group/all-generations-program.

[12] "Allianz Engage - Our Employee Network for Age Inclusion." Allianz. https://www.allianz.com/en/about-us/strategy-values/diversity/allianz_engage.html.

[13] "Fostering a Culture of Diversity, Inclusion, and Innovation." Allianz People Fact Book 2022. Allianz SE, April 5, 2023. https://www.allianz.com/en/mediacenter/news/company/human_resources/230405_Allianz-People-Fact-Book-2022-Fostering-a-culture-of-diversity-inclusion-and-innovation.html.

[14] MacroTrends. "U.S. Life Expectancy 1950-2025." https://www.macrotrends.net/global-metrics/countries/USA/united-states/life-expectancy.

[15] "Employee Tenure in 2024." Bureau of Labor Statistics. U.S. Department of Labor, September 26, 2026. https://www.bls.gov/news.release/pdf/tenure.pdf.

[16] Borden, Taylor. "Most Americans Are Taking Time off This Summer — but Not Fully Unplugging. See the Data Behind the Nation's Vacation Culture.," August 19, 2024. https://www.linkedin.com/pulse/most-americans-taking-time-off-summer-fully-see-data-behind-borden-anbyf.

[17] Boushy, Brandon. "47 Best Side Hustle Ideas (for 2024)." UpFlip. October 24, 2023. https://www.upflip.com/blog/side-hustle-ideas.

[18] Latu, Dan. "Teacher Found a Lucrative Side Hustle Decorating College Kids' Dorm Rooms." Business Insider,

August 23, 2024. https://www.businessinsider.com/teacher-side-hustle-getting-paid-design-decorate-college-dorm-rooms-2024-8.
[19] Zapier Editorial Team. "Zapier Report: 40% of Americans Have a Side Hustle in 2022," June 7, 2022. https://zapier.com/blog/side-hustle-report-2022.
[20] McKinsey & Company. "What Is the Gig Economy?," August 2, 2023. https://www.mckinsey.com/featured-insights/mckinsey-explainers/what-is-the-gig-economy.
[21] MBO Partners study.
[22] Kreisberg, Nicole. "New Careers for Older Workers." AIER, September 8, 2015. https://aier.org/wp-content/uploads/2015/09/newcareersolderworkers-aier.pdf.
[23] Norris-Tirrell, Dorothy, Ph.D., Jennifer Rinella Ed.D. CNP, Xuan Pham Ph.D, and Gene Moses MPA, CNP. "Who Is at the Top in the Social Sector? Examining Career Paths of Nonprofit Executive Leaders." Nonprofit Leadership Alliance, April 17, 2017. https://www.nonprofitleadershipalliance.org/wp-content/uploads/2017/04/CEO-Research-Initial-Release-2.pdf.
[24] Yakoboski, Paul J. "Adjunct faculty: Who they are and what is their experience?" TIAA Institute, November 2018. https://www.tiaa.org/content/dam/tiaa/institute/pdf/insights-report/2019-07/tiaa-institute-2018-adjunct-faculty-survey-november-2018.pdf.
[25] Wells, Tom. "Franchise Statistics 2023: Uncovering Insights for Entrepreneurs." Marketing Scoop, April 21, 2024. https://www.marketingscoop.com/consumer/franchise-statistics/.
[26] "2024 S&P 500 New Director and Diversity Snapshot," August 2024. https://www.spencerstuart.com/research-and-insight/sp-500-new-director-and-diversity-snapshot.

Chapter 7: Wealth

[1] Williams, Geoff. "How to Calculate Your Net Worth." U.S. News & World Report, September 26, 2024. https://money.

usnews.com/money/personal-finance/saving-and-budgeting/
articles/how-to-calculate-your-net-worth.

[2] "Everyday Wealth in America || 2023 Report: The Intersection
of Life and Money." Edelman Financial Engines, n.d. https://
www.edelmanfinancialengines.com/content/dam/efe/
corporate-brand/production-web-assets/downloadable-content/
everyday-wealth-in-america-reports/Everyday-Wealth-in-
America-2023.pdf.

[3] "Schwab Modern Wealth Survey." Charles
Schwab, June 2023. https://www.aboutschwab.com/
schwab-modern-wealth-survey-2023.

[4] Cerulli Associates. "Cerulli | Press Release: Cerulli
Anticipates $84 Trillion in Wealth Transfers Through 2045,"
January 20, 2022. https://www.cerulli.com/press-releases/
cerulli-anticipates-84-trillion-in-wealth-transfers-through-2045.

[5] Wealth-X. "A Generational Shift: Family Wealth Transfer
Report 2019 - Wealth-X," February 12, 2024. https://wealthx.
com/reports/wealth-transfer-report-2019.

[6] Silver, Caleb. "Lessons From the 2008 Financial Crisis."
Investopedia, September 13, 2023. https://www.investopedia.
com/news/10-years-later-lessons-financial-crisis.

[7] Bank of America Private Bank Study of Wealthy Americans,
2022.

[8] Bank of America Private Bank Study of Wealthy Americans,
2024. https://www.privatebank.bankofamerica.com/articles/
generational-divide-wealth-study.html

[9] Envestnet. "Intelligent Financial Life - National Study."
Envestnet. https://www.envestnet.com/intelligent-financial-life/
national-study.

[10] Lazarowitz, Elizabeth. "Money Dysmorphia." *The New York
Times*, June 30, 2024. https://www.nytimes.com/2024/06/28/
business/what-is-money-dysmorphia.html.

[11] "Everyday Wealth in America || 2023 Report: The Intersection
of Life and Money." Edelman Financial Engines, n.d. https://

www.edelmanfinancialengines.com/content/dam/efe/
corporate-brand/production-web-assets/downloadable-content/
everyday-wealth-in-america-reports/Everyday-Wealth-in-
America-2023.pdf.

[12] Frías Portfolio Management Group. "Visualizing
$156 trillion in U.S. assets, by generation,"
August 17, 2023. https://santiagofrias.com/
visualizing-156-trillion-in-u-s-assets-by-generation.

[13] "FinTech Market Overview With Size, Share, Value | Growth
[2032]," December 2024. https://www.fortunebusinessinsights.
com/fintech-market-108641.

[14] Alkami Technology Inc. "Generational Trends in
Digital Banking Study." Alkami Technology » Digital
Banking Solutions for Banks and Credit Unions, May
22, 2024. https://alkamidev.wpengine.com/resource/
generational-trends-in-digital-banking-study.

[15] Raynor, Lilah. "Don't You Forget About Us: Gen X And
The Future of Money." The Financial Brand, March 31,
2023. https://thefinancialbrand.com/news/bank-marketing/
gen-x-insights-how-they-make-spend-invest-money-159039.

[16] iSpot.tv | Realtime TV Advertising Performance
Measurement. "JPMorgan Chase TV Spot, 'Meet
the Jennifers,'" n.d. https://www.ispot.tv/ad/5wEp/
jpmorgan-chase-banking-meet-the-jennifers.

[17] Envestnet. "Intelligent Financial Life - National Study |
Envestnet." https://www.envestnet.com/intelligent-financial-life/
national-study.

[18] Ibid

[19] Dugan, Mary Ellen, and Jason Dorsey. "The Intelligent
Financial Life National Study." Evestnet, 2022. https://
www.envestnet.com/sites/default/files/documents/
the-intelligent-financial-life-national-study-envestnet-2022.
pdf?utm_source=pardot&utm_medium=form&utm_
content=whitepaper&utm_campaign=ifl_website.

[20] Adam, Jamela. "Millennials and Generation Z Are More Likely to Discuss Salary Than Older Generations." Forbes Advisor, September 29, 2023. https://www.forbes.com/advisor/banking/talking-about-money-by-generation.

[21] Hallez, Emile. "Gen X Could Get Trillions in Inheritance Over 10 Years." Investment News, July 3, 2024. https://www.investmentnews.com/retirement-planning/gen-x-could-get-trillions-in-inheritance-over-10-years/254961.

[22] Baghai, Pooneh, Olivia Howard, Lakshmi Prakash, and Jill Zucker. "Women as the Next Wave of Growth in US Wealth Management." McKinsey & Company, July 29, 2020. https://www.mckinsey.com/industries/financial-services/our-insights/women-as-the-next-wave-of-growth-in-us-wealth-management.

Chapter 8: Wellness

[1] International Health, Racquet & Sportsclub Association (IHRSA), 2023.

[2] American College of Sports Medicine, 2023.

[3] Elgaddal, Nazik, Ellen A. Kramarow, and Cynthia Reuben. "Physical Activity Among Adults Aged 18 and Over: United States, 2020." National Center for Health Statistics, August 2022. https://doi.org/10.15620/cdc:120213.

[4] Yoga Alliance, 2022.

[5] Sports & Fitness Industry Association (SFIA), 2023.

[6] Blazina, Carrie. "About One-in-five Americans Use a Smart Watch or Fitness Tracker." Pew Research Center, April 14, 2024. https://www.pewresearch.org/short-reads/2020/01/09/about-one-in-five-americans-use-a-smart-watch-or-fitness-tracker.

[7] International Food Information Council, 2023.

[8] Nutrigenomix Study.

[9] "Global $1.39 Bn Nutrigenomics Markets to 2026 - Increasing Demand for Nutritious and Healthy Food Alternatives and Consumers Shifting Toward Healthier Food."

GlobeNewswire News Room, March 31, 2022. https://www.globenewswire.com/news-release/2022/03/31/2413562/0/en/Global-1-39-Bn-Nutrigenomics-Markets-to-2026-Increasing-Demand-for-Nutritious-and-Healthy-Food-Alternatives-and-Consumers-Shifting-Toward-Healthier-Food.html.

[10] International Food Information Council. 2024 Food & Health Survey. June 20, 2024. https://foodinsight.org/2024-foodhealth-survey.

[11] "Kombucha Market Size, Industry Share, Growth Analysis, Forecast," December 23, 2024. https://www.fortunebusinessinsights.com/industry-reports/kombucha-market-100230.

[12] American Academy of Dermatology, 2023.

[13] Research, Precedence. "Anti-aging Market Size to Worth Around US$ 119.6 Bn by 2030." GlobeNewswire News Room, March 29, 2022. https://www.globenewswire.com/news-release/2022/03/29/2412093/0/en/Anti-aging-Market-Size-to-Worth-Around-US-119-6-Bn-by-2030.html.

[14] "Stress in America™ 2023: A Nation Grappling With Psychological Impacts of Collective Trauma," November 1, 2023. https://www.apa.org/news/press/releases/2023/11/psychological-impacts-collective-trauma.

[15] National Center for Complementary and Integrative Health, 2023.

[16] Dawkins, Megan. "FlexJobs Report: Workplace Perspectives of a Multigenerational Workforce." FlexJobs Job Search Tips and Blog (blog), July 19, 2024. https://www.flexjobs.com/blog/post/flexjobs-report-workplace-perspectives-of-a-multigenerational-workforce.

[17] National Sleep Foundation.

[18] NielsenIQ. "Gen Z Alcohol Trends - NIQ." NIQ, October 11, 2024. https://nielseniq.com/global/en/insights/analysis/2024/gen-z-alcohol-trends.

[19] "Global Non-Alcoholic Beer Market Report 2021: Market is Expected to Reach $23.27 Billion in 2025 at a CAGR of 8.7% - Forecast to 2030," BusinessWire, January 4, 2022. https://www.businesswire.com/news/home/20220104005772/en/Global-Non-Alcoholic-Beer-Market-Report-2021-Market-is-Expected-to-Reach-23.27-Billion-in-2025-at-a-CAGR-of-8.7.

[20] Accenture, 2023.

[21] Knowles, Madelyn, Adriana Krasniansky, and Ashwini Nagappan. "Consumer Adoption of Digital Health in 2022: Moving at the Speed of Trust." Rock Health, February 21, 2023. https://rockhealth.com/insights/consumer-adoption-of-digital-health-in-2022-moving-at-the-speed-of-trust.

Chapter 9: Gen Xers Living Their Best Lives

[1] Degn, Emily Iris. "Globally, Gen X Spending More on Luxury Trips Than Any Other Age Group: McKinsey." Luxury Daily, June 3, 2024. https://www.luxurydaily.com/globally-gen-x-spending-more-on-luxury-trips-than-any-other-age-group-mckinsey.

[2] Bain & Company, 2023.

[3] National Association of Realtors.

[4] Deloitte, 2023.

[5] Consumer Technology Association, 2023.

[6] SuperData Research, 2023.

[7] Global Wellness Institute, 2023.

[8] Equinox Holdings, Inc., Annual Report, 2023,

[9] Adventure Travel Trade Association Wellness Tourism Report.

[10] Williams-Sonoma Annual Report, 2023.

[11] Wine Market Council Consumer Segmentation Study, 2023.

[12] American Craft Spirits Association Market Report, 2023.

[13] Blue Apron Holdings, Inc. Q4 2023 Earnings Call transcript.

Chapter 10: Gen Xcellerators

[1] Green, Ricki. "Indeed.com Launches 'How the World Works' Global Brand Campaign in Australia via Mullen." Campaign Brief, October 30, 2014. https://campaignbrief.com/indeedcom-launches-how-the-wor/. Fun fact!: "How the World Works" was an Indeed brand campaign spearheaded by the author Mary Ellen Dugan in 2014–2015.

[2] https://truebridgenetwork.com/what-we-do

[3] LPL Financial. "LPL Financial to Acquire Atria Wealth Solutions," February 13, 2024. https://www.lpl.com/news-media/press-releases/lpl-financial-to-acquire-atria-wealth-solutions.html.

[4] Holcomb, Bob. "The Personalization Equation." Atria Wealth Solutions, December 4, 2023. https://atriawealth.com/how-we-think/the-personalization-equation.

[5] "Fidelity Investments, 2020 Highlights." Fidelity. https://www.fidelity.com/bin-public/060_www_fidelity_com/documents/about-fidelity/Fidelity_Investments_2020_Annual_Report_Infographic.pdf.

[6] "Fidelity Annual Report, 2023." Fidelity, n.d. https://www.fidelity.com/bin-public/060_www_fidelity_com/documents/about-fidelity/2023-Fidelity-Investments-Annual-Report.pdf.

Supplemental Links for Additional Reading

Introduction: X Marks the Spot
- https://www.investopedia.com/terms/g/generation-x-genx.asp
- https://www.responsemedia.com/spending-across-generations-gen-xers-shop

Chapter 1: Who Is Gen X?
- https://www.linkedin.com/in/jasondorsey
- *North American Journal of Psychology*, 2010
- https://www.nar.realtor/research-and-statistics/research-reports/home-buyer-and-seller-generational-trends
- https://www.the-future-of-commerce.com/2023/11/01/generation-x-definition-years-stats-work-spending-trends

Chapter 3: Money Matters
- https://www.empower.com/the-currency/money/emergency-fund-how-much-should-i-save
- https://www.brookings.edu/articles/economic-mobility-of-families-across-generations

Chapter 10: Gen Xcellerators
- https://www.fidelity.com/learning-center/personal-finance/gen-x-retirement-guide

About the Authors

Mary Ellen Dugan and Julia Fitzgerald are award-winning CMOs who have built and grown B2B and B2C brands across companies ranging from $55M to $15B in revenue. They've accelerated growth for iconic brands including Build-A-Bear, Dell Technologies, Envestnet, Hallmark, Indeed, Kmart, VTech, WP Engine, and more.

Lifelong friends who met at The Ohio State University, Mary Ellen earned her MBA from NYU's Stern School of Business and Julia from Northwestern's Kellogg School of Management. Mary Ellen is the producer of *makeSHIFT*, a documentary on digital trends, and has conducted four generational studies. Julia authored the Amazon bestseller *Midsize*, offering marketing strategies for mid-market growth.

United by their shared expertise in uncovering untapped opportunities, Mary Ellen and Julia bring complementary perspectives and proven strategies to help businesses leverage Gen X's influence as consumers, culture shapers, and economic powerhouses.

Made in United States
Troutdale, OR
03/26/2025

30104132R00149